COLLISION COURSE

COLLISION COURSE

*How to Harness
the Power of Love to Heal
Your Broken Life*

BARRY FERGUSON

New York

COLLISION COURSE

How to Harness the Power of Love to Heal Your Broken Life

Published in New York, New York, by Morgan James Publishing. Morgan James and The Entrepreneurial Publisher are trademarks of Morgan James, LLC. www.MorganJamesPublishing.com

The Morgan James Speakers Group can bring authors to your live event. For more information or to book an event visit The Morgan James Speakers Group at www.TheMorganJamesSpeakersGroup.com.

Find more information at: www.BarryFergusonAuthor.com

A **free** eBook edition is available
with the purchase of this print book.

CLEARLY PRINT YOUR NAME ABOVE IN UPPER CASE

Instructions to claim your free eBook edition:
1. Download the Shelfie app for Android or iOS
2. Write your name in **UPPER CASE** above
3. Use the Shelfie app to submit a photo
4. Download your eBook to any device

ISBN 978-1-63047-940-4 paperback
ISBN 978-1-63047-942-8 eBook
ISBN 978-1-63047-941-1 hardcover
Library of Congress Control Number:
2016900352

Cover Design by:
Rachel Lopez
www.r2cdesign.com

Interior Design by:
Bonnie Bushman
The Whole Caboodle Graphic Design

In an effort to support local communities, raise awareness and funds, Morgan James Publishing donates a percentage of all book sales for the life of each book to Habitat for Humanity Peninsula and Greater Williamsburg.

Get involved today! Visit
www.MorganJamesBuilds.com

DEDICATION

This book is dedicated to all those people who stood by me during my hour of need, especially my family and friends. We don't know what we have until we lose it and I could not bear to lose those so precious to me before my time on earth was up.

I would also like to dedicate this book to Jesus Christ, my Lord and Savior, for bringing me back from the depths of despair and for saving my life. You have put me on this planet for a reason and I finally realized what that reason is. May I be able to do your will as you see fit.

TABLE OF CONTENTS

INTRODUCTION

"Trust is the first step to love."
—Munshi Premchand

Love is the most important part of everyone's life. There is not a person alive who can say they do not aspire to love and be loved. It's the strongest of human emotions and when we are lacking love in our life, we feel so alone.

This is my story of transformational love. I have written this book as a way for you to unlock your potential to love. I know firsthand what it feels like to be unhappy, unloved, and uncared for but I've discovered proven secrets to help you overcome your own past and heal your broken life.

Many people have been inspired by my story and have asked me to write a book outlining how I overcame so much to become such a magnet for love. We all share many of the same hurts and painful memories yet most people do not know how to heal the past sorrows and grief and end up living with sadness deep inside their hearts.

This book is part three of a trilogy that has brought me full circle in my quest to find the true meaning of love.

Book one is entitled, **"Summoned To Love – A Spiritual Blueprint For Rediscovering Peace, Love, And Happiness In All Areas Of your Life."** This is what we are called to do… love others. It's the only way to find peace, love, and happiness.

Book two is entitled, **"Love Goggles – How To Heal Your Inner Blindness By Mastering The Art Of Unconditional Love."** It is what we are all guilty of… Deception By Perception.

After reading this book, you are going to be able to heal your past wounds, understand how to experience the true nature of love, and how to bring more love into your life. Not only that, you will be able to focus the incredible power of the love you already have inside in such a way that happiness will become second nature to you

Throughout this book I reveal some golden nuggets from my life where I give you examples of my transformation and how it can inspire you to transform your own life. I have also included a myriad of quotes and messages from people who have influenced me to help guide you along your path.

But the most important parts of this book show you how messed up my life was before the accident. I include the bitter truth, warts and all to make you see that you don't have to be perfect… you just have to be yourself.

I have studied various techniques from people far more experienced than myself in a quest to change my life. The ideas I have learned have given me a new perspective on the root causes of both my unhappiness and the reasons why we act the way we do.

Look, this world needs all the love it can get. There is too much war, too much hate, and far too much suffering going on so wouldn't it be nice if we could add just a little more love and happiness into our own lives?

This is your challenge… go out and spread the gift of love everywhere you go. It can only make everyone's life that much better. Spreading love and joy has become a passion of mine and I want you to experience it the same way I have… with an unselfish heart that is full of sincere gratitude.

THE COLLISION

"Being deeply loved by someone gives you strength,
while loving someone deeply gives you courage."
—Lao Tzu

O n September 13, 2014, my life as I knew it was changed forever. While driving to work as a letter carrier early on a Saturday morning, I was nearly killed in a horrifying car accident.

My 2010 Chevrolet Equinox was broadsided by a car that had run a red light. My SUV flipped over numerous times and rolled approximately forty feet down the street. The police and EMS had to tear me out of the car through the sun roof as the SUV dangled precariously on its side.

During the accident, all I could think about was my family. Never seeing them again scared the living hell out of me. Even though the accident took less than a few seconds, it felt like a lifetime. Everything seemed to happen in slow motion. A million thoughts raced through my head as I prayed for my life.

It was such a surreal event. Initially, I was in shock and thought I came out of it with just a few bumps and bruises but the lingering effects will be with me for a lifetime.

Six weeks later, on November 4th, the unthinkable happened again. While driving home after picking up my youngest daughter from her soccer practice at around seven in the evening, I was involved in yet another horrible accident.

The car, which I had just purchased two weeks earlier, was completely totaled. Both my daughter and I survived (thank God) but the painful experience of almost dying again really affected me. Although neither accident was my fault (police reports and a successful court appearance will back me up on this), it led me down a deep, dark path of depression. I tried to hide it from everyone (including my family) but it got to be too much for me to bear.

Four herniated and crushed discs in my back, two in my neck, and three successive surgeries later have resulted in physical pain that will last me for the rest of my life but it's the emotional nightmare that I will never live down. These are the sad remnants of the two accidents but one nagging question kept going through my mind since the crash.

"If I had died, could I honestly say that I gave more love than I received?"

Sadly, the answer to this question took me several months to figure out (I guess I didn't want to accept the awful truth) while I went through a grueling physical therapy. Though I only missed a few days of work during that time, I couldn't get the idea of love out of my head.

Trying to figure out why my life was spared when others weren't so lucky was something I couldn't fathom at the time. I was alive yet most of me felt dead inside. I believe it was love that saved my life.

You may scoff at the idea of love being my savior but it's true. I've gone through a complete transformation and I'm at peace with myself and my past.

This led me on to a search… a quest for truth and why love had ultimately saved me.

I really wanted to know why so many people like me find it hard to attract love into their lives. I'm not talking about sexual love or the love of attracting a mate. Instead, I examined the idea of people caring for one another and living a life based more on loving others than serving one's own selfish needs.

What really bugged me was the fact I saw so much hate and anger in the world and I felt I was part of it. I decided to change my life, my thinking, and my habits and start giving more love back than I took. This book is my attempt to come to grips with myself.

I have studied and read so many books on the true meaning of love, Googled thousands of articles about how to love others, and watched video after video till I couldn't see straight and then tried to figure out how a loser like myself could become a lightning rod for love.

I boiled it all down to 3 main steps and decided to write a book that would help others attract more love into their own lives while at the same time showing them how to love others more deeply. Love healed my life and I want you to be healed as well.

YOU CAN'T
HIDE ANYMORE

"Love, we say, is life; but love without hope
and faith is agonizing death."
—Elbert Hubbard

What do you see when you look in the mirror?

Do you see the real you or some distorted funhouse mirror version of yourself? In my mind, the twisted version of who I was ruled my every thought. No matter where I went I felt I could never measure up to what I wanted to be. What I saw when I looked in the mirror made me sick to my stomach!

My negative thoughts did me in. I couldn't get the negativity out of my head. I would replay the day's events in my mind when I went to sleep, going over all the things I did wrong, getting mad at those who hurt me, and praying that I could be saved from the horror that was my everyday life. On the outside I looked like everyone else but on the inside I was slowly dying a miserable and horrible death.

Have you ever felt so alone in the world that when you walked into a room you could literally blow yourself up and no one would ever notice? Ever wonder that if you died tomorrow not a soul would show up to your funeral?

This was my life prior to my car accident. I felt like nothing I did mattered to anyone. My life was a mess. I had few friends and I was a failure at everything I seem to get my hands on.

I was stuck in a dead end job for the past twenty-eight years with no real hope of leaving, had no money, was over $45,000 in debt with my business and my wife and I had amassed a personal credit card debt of over $16,000.

I saw no way out of my problems but I persevered on because I had a dream. My dream was to be an author. To write books that changed people's lives. I was an author who mostly wrote children's adventure stories but I couldn't sell enough to make it work. In fact, I couldn't even give them away.

You see, I love kids! There's nothing better than listening to a child talk about a book they just read and to see the joy on their faces. I enjoy working with kids and teaching them how to come up with great story ideas and then put those ideas on paper.

I had hoped to make an impact in this world but I was barely getting by. My heart was in the right place but little did I know that my mind needed a jolt and boy did it ever happen!

Sometimes, God tries to get our attention and we don't listen very well. Other times, God waits for us to come to him even when we think we know everything. In my case, God decided it was my time for a wakeup call.

To comprehend the full impact of nearly dying in such a devastating way cannot be fully understood unless you have experienced it for yourself! Only then can you get inside the heart and mind of someone who has cheated death... not once but twice!

Some have said I was just plain lucky while others have told me it wasn't my time and that got me thinking. If it wasn't my time then what kind of legacy can I leave behind when it is my time? What can I do for others that will show my love for this world?

We all have a certain amount of time on this planet and if we don't contribute to the happiness of others while we're still here then what have we accomplished? Have we done anything to improve the lives of others?

I have felt so alone for so long that I didn't think my story mattered. I was running from life even though I had big dreams.

What are your dreams? Are they selfish in nature or do you have a plan to make this world a better place?

Did you know you have an enormous gift hiding deep within you? A big, bold, beautiful gift that can change the world! It's true but you have to be willing to accept it on faith.

Running away from everything is not the answer. I know because it doesn't get you anywhere. It's not that you're running from something but it's where you're running to that's the real problem. Your problems may be killing you inside but where you are going is even worse! It's like running from the mouth of a lion into the waiting jaws of a shark with no place to hide.

We all have our own horror stories to tell but everyone's story matters! Just because you haven't been heard before doesn't mean no one cares. I felt that way all my life until I found out just how much God cares. He showed me where I was going wrong with my life. He showed me I had worth and that what I did truly mattered.

The day I had my accident was the worst day I ever experienced or so I believed... but when I sit down and look at it from a new perspective, I realize it was the best thing that ever happened to me.

Why? Because the way I was going I was headed for a major fall. I don't mean I was going to die by taking drugs or abusing alcohol but I was so unhappy that I felt I would have just faded away from existence without anyone ever knowing I had ever lived.

Is there something inside you yearning to come out? Do you feel like you have something you want to express? It can be yours but the first thing you must do is stop running away. There's no place you can go that can save you. It's all deep inside your heart.

I had such a hard time believing that my life mattered. I know my family loved me but what about other people? I felt so alone in this world but guess what? God was in my corner and I wasn't using his unconditional love to my full advantage.

Now, when I meet new people I have a sense of urgency to help bring change to those that are hurting and a chance at peace for those who need it. When you experience what love has to offer you will never want to go back to your old way of life. It doesn't have to take a car accident to wake you up like it did me... only the love of a fellow human being who wants to help you turn your life around and see the beauty that God has given each one of us.

Which path do you want your life to follow?

Do you really want to remain in the pain you are feeling or are you willing to start all over and make a difference? Learn from my mistakes (I have made a hell of a lot of them) and become the person that God wants you to be! Be the person *YOU* have always wanted to be.

I didn't think it was possible for me to change my circumstances but I'm not running anymore! My feet are firmly planted on the ground and I have a reason to go on. I really don't care what others think of me or what they do to because I have a passion for life. God is there walking beside me and is guiding my every move. He has opened up the door to a life that is full of love and hope. A life that you can have… if you really want it!

Love has always there but your eyes were closed to it as mine once were.

Let me show you how to start loving more and how to be loved more. Let me help you see yourself in a brand new way. A way filled with hope, love, and a new direction.

I do love you! Those are not some words I wrote just to get you on my side. I really do mean it! It's up to you to open your heart to both me and everyone else you know. Stop running and start loving. Stop hiding and start living. I've done it and so can you.

Does the idea of being loved scare you?

Don't worry about that. Instead, take a chance and experience the joy that life has to offer. Just say yes and your journey will begin.

HEALING YOUR
HEART AND SOUL

*"Blessed is the influence of one true,
loving human soul on another."*
—George Eliot

W hen you are sick you need healing. But when your life is a mess, where do you go for healing? How many times have you said to yourself, I wish my life was better? I wish I had more money, more friends, a better job, less bills, etc.?

Before you can receive any of those things you need to heal your heart and your soul first. Together they make up who you are and how you function in this world.

But why are those two things so special? Why should we focus on them when the problems in our lives are so severe?

Unhappiness was my biggest problem. It forced me to hide myself from life. I was bitter, angry, and felt so unloved and I blocked all attempts at trying to fix my heart and soul because the pain was so great. I walked around like a zombie wishing I could be happy but I refused to go out of my comfort zone because I was so afraid of change. I didn't think I could be "fixed" and made whole again.

The heart is the window to the soul. Seeking to fix what is within us is one of life's greatest challenges. We put up so many walls around us that fixing our heart takes so many steps. We tear down one wall only to find an even bigger one waiting behind it.

When healing doesn't come quick enough we give up before we have the chance to reach a certain level of happiness that can spur us on to greater things in our lives. So what do we do? We run away and hide. Hide from everything that we think is causing our pain.

We all have our secret hurts. Those hurts that ache for healing but never get it. The aches which we have endured our whole lives and have closed off parts of ourselves to ease the suffering. It is these aches that you need to focus on because they are the ones that cause you the most pain.

Healing our hearts and souls from past afflictions is all based on forgiving ourselves first. **Russell Bishop**, an educational psychologist, author, consultant and executive coach, has a unique take on the subject.

He states that *"Self-forgiveness stems from the realization that whatever you might have done, or even whatever the other person might have done, has less to do with the action itself, but more with the judgment you have placed against yourself for judging in the first place. Judging anyone, yourself included, is a source of great pain because judging denies the Divinity of both yourself and the other person."*

We are all divine beings. We are all children of God yet we deny our divinity in such a way that we separate ourselves from the peace in our souls. That separation causes pain. When we are in pain we lash out just like any animal would.

Seek the peace that emanates from within your heart and soul. Find that special place where you can feel safe first. In this place, work from a center of calmness. Concentrate on the restless part of your mind that is holding you back from forgiving yourself.

In this world, calmness is a dirty word. We seem to be busy 24/7 yet we get nothing done. We complain there is no time to do anything but continuously search for more to do. What we are actually doing is trying to quiet all the noise going on in our own hearts and souls.

Stop attacking your mind with so many stimulations and concentrate on those things that offer peace and quiet. Everything else is just peripheral commotion and does nothing to make your life any better.

Feeling love makes you vulnerable to getting hurt but it is in that love that you can be made whole again. There is so much love deep within you trying to come out. You were created from love and you are made up of love. Even your soul is a bastion of love!

If you a seek healing, you must find it within yourself. You cannot go forward without healing your past. This quote by **Marianne Williamson** sums it up. *"We do not heal the past by dwelling there; we heal the past by living fully in the present."*

Our present is all we have. This is my story. My accident almost wiped out my present and my future but I realized I had a choice to make. I could remain wallowing in my own misery or open up to what life had to offer and receive it with open arms.

Like a hungry and sick child we need to breathe nourishment back into our hearts and revive our souls with the delights of our senses. Delight them with such things as the feeling of the wind through your hair, the smell of flowers on a beautiful spring day, and the taste of a delicious meal.

Beating ourselves up with our own problems prohibits us from experiencing the beauty of life. Yes, you are going to have problems. It's something we all go through but I didn't say everything would be perfect. Isn't it better to feel life than to hide from the pain, to let the problems turn us into shells of ourselves?

Running is not the answer. Neither is hiding in your room trying to get away from life. I believe you have to experience life in order to really live it.

Heather Rees is a career change coach who states, *"For every pain, there is a pleasure. And I suspect that we are capable of pleasures far beyond the reaches of any pain."*

We look for things to take the place of our pain instead of finding things to be our pleasure. Drugs, alcohol and sex cannot replace true pleasure. They cannot heal our hearts and our spirits. The spirit flies when we give it wings not when we launch it into the air without a way for it to move forward.

I used to beat myself up every time I made a mistake or felt like I wasn't good enough in any given situation. Now, I look at each new circumstance as a new way to experience life and the rewards it has to offer.

I look for the goodness in others whether they can see it or not in themselves. I have calmed my inner spirit so that I can see the love around me. It wasn't easy but I do my best to be a witness for God's love.

Paramahansa Yogananda, one of the preeminent spiritual leaders of the twentieth century and author of the best-selling classic book, **"Autobiography Of A Yogi"** asks us to find peace in this affirmation which states, *"I will mingle my inner devotional whispers with the prayers of all saints, and continuously offer them in the temple of silence and activity until I hear God loudly whispering from everywhere."*

If you are too busy feeling sorry for yourself and cannot see what life is offering you then you cannot hear the loud whispers of God as he calls you to his peace.

I am my own individual person yet I live to help others. I try to bring the message of peace and love to all but I've learned from **Paramahansa Yognanda** who said it much better than I could ever say, *"The happiness of one's own heart alone cannot satisfy the soul; one must try to include, as necessary to one's own happiness, the happiness of others."*

If you live to serve you will find the peace of a calm soul and the way to healing your heart and soul. To take it further, **Paramahansa** asks us to do this: *"Let my soul smile through my heart and my heart smile through my eyes, that I may scatter rich smiles in sad hearts."*

There is nothing to gain from a sad heart and an empty soul. Fill it with love and care and look to help others heal their pain. In doing so, we do the work that God asks of us in **Matthew 5:14-16**, *"You are the light of the world. A city set on a hill cannot be hidden. Nor do people light a lamp and put it under a basket, but on a stand, and it gives light to all in the house. In the same way, let your light shine before others, so that they may see your good works and give glory to your Father who is in heaven."*

That glory is what heals your broken heart and brings joy to a lonely soul. The pathway has been revealed, now take the map and be on your way.

FINDING TRANSFORMATIONAL HEALING WITH LOVE

"The greatest healing therapy is friendship and love."
—Hubert H. Humphrey

How do you transfer your life from chaos to peace? How do you transform your pain into love? How do you shift from fear to self-acceptance.?

Transformation begins the moment you believe you are loved. When you open yourself up to love then happiness will follow. Love is and always will be the key!

Our bodies are the mirrors of our inner thought process and what we are physically feeling at any given time is a direct manifestation of that release of either positive or negative energy. Focus on the positive release of energy and you begin the healing process.

Why transformative healing?

Healing our pain, our sinful tendencies, and our past is not just a part of our life, it is the change needed to complete who we really are. It changes us and brings us to a place where we can truly live in harmony and peace.

Happiness is what love gives us but without it, we cannot become the person we were meant to be. Rather than us focusing on adding things that can make us happy, isn't it better to look at what causes us to be unhappy and either change or remove them so that we can focus on being loved?

For years, I tried to look for happiness instead of getting rid of the garbage in my life. I stuck with friends through thick and thin even though they brought me down. All they did was moan and complain about life and I got caught up in that type of negative attitude. Only when I removed the real source of my unhappiness did some sense of serenity return. It was painful losing a friend but was he really a true friend if all he did was bring us both down?

Love for all the wrong reasons is not love. We are our own worst enemies yet we cling to relationships that damage us. You can still love the person but you need to break free and find your own true happiness.

Did you know that most of our physical and emotional traumas are due to a damaged spirit? We need to re-connect to a place where both truth and love co-exist and where emptiness is replaced by the guiding hand of God.

Our hearts are vessels of love which are filled by the grace of God. It is in our suffering that we see God for who he is. His love is the miracle that works in our lives.

Albert Einstein once said: *"There are only two ways to live your life. One is as though nothing is a miracle. The other is as though everything is a miracle."*

If we see everything as gift from God we have the foundation to love. We can begin the transformational healing that God has given us.

Awareness is the first step in healing. Being aware that we have a loving God who wants the best for us changes our focus from being self-centered to God-centered. The power that God gives us can be seen in what he did for us. God is the source of all love and helps facilitate the healing we need with his unconditional love.

Don't think you're loved?

Think again. There are so many stories of people with this type of thinking who find out just how wrong they are. Here's an example below.

I met a woman at a writer's conference who told me the story of a beautiful young Indian lady who was on the brink of committing suicide. She was in an arranged marriage where the husband didn't want nor loved her. He beat her constantly and mistreated her to the point that she had no self worth. She had nowhere to go and was incredibly miserable.

This woman intervened and took her into her home. She fed her, took care of her and showed her unconditional love. The young lady finally realized how loved she was and found the strength to carry on. She was able to reunite with her husband later on after he promised to go to counseling and rehab and now they have a beautiful baby. She is doing well both emotionally and physically because she saw what love can do. Her life changed because someone was willing to give her unconditional love.

It is never too late to help someone in need by being that transformational healer. It only takes one person to help another. You never know what you mean to another unless you show that love. Healing begins when you inject love into someone's life.

For most people, they get this all wrong. They are always looking to receive love. But if you're always looking for love from someone else you are only getting half the picture. Love is a two way street. You must give as well as receive. It's a delicate balance. The more you give the more you receive. It balances out when you change your perspective.

Eric Alsterberg, author of the book, **"Life Is an Adventure: A Guide to the Path of Joy"** writes this about love, *"Approaching life from only one part of the mind not only denies the intuitive part, but also the greater foundation of a mind based on the positive, love-based emotions from the heart. We are meant to operate from the heart to the mind."*

Often, we feel very different from others and because we are lonely and frightened, we don't invite healing into our lives. That's the key here, inviting a healing that can transform our lives. Love brings the most powerful healing energy known to man and is a catalyst for transforming our hearts and our souls.

Our inability to love ourselves causes us to shy away from loving others but we can heal ourselves when we open our hearts to love despite our perceptions of feeling betrayed, abandoned, humiliated, and rejected by our past.

Our willingness to begin the healing is essential in bringing back peace into our lives. Healing enables harmony in our hearts which promotes trust regardless of what we are experiencing. It gives us permission to be ourselves and the freedom and self-determination to become the person we want to be.

My transformation from a scared and lonely person with no confidence to a caring and loving person who trusts in the healing power of God's love is well documented in this book. If I can change you most certainly can. If I can love so can you.

Do you want those possibilities in your life?

Courage is being able to transform your life even if there seems no hope in sight. You are what you believe so if you believe there is hope, transformation begins. This is your possibility.

LIVING WITH YOUR
GREATEST PASSION

*"There is no passion to be found in settling for a life
that is less than the one you are capable of living."*
—Nelson Mandela

W hat is your greatest passion in life?
Finding your passion increases your ability to love. That ability is your greatest asset. If you are just drifting through life without a purpose then finding that purpose is your main goal.

Living your passion was very important to **Howard Thurman**, an influential African American author, philosopher, theologian and educator. He made it his life work to instill those values in people, especially in his writings. He once wrote, *"Don't ask yourself what the world needs. Ask yourself what makes you come alive, and then go and do that. Because what the world needs is people who have come alive."*

It's never too late to find that purpose and to begin living a life filled with excitement and motivation.

Do you know what it feels like to wake up in the morning and feel alive? To know what you are doing is actually making a real difference in the world!

If not, ask yourself why and be honest. Are you making excuses for yourself? Do you just exist instead of really living life to the fullest?

Have you found a passion that makes *YOU* happy?

It can't be because of a lack of money as money does not buy passion. It can't be because you haven't been given the talent. You have all the talent you need right inside of you. It is God given.

What is holding you back?

Are you scared that someone may laugh at you? Do you feel you are not good enough? You only believe you aren't good enough. **Selena Soo**, a business strategist, publicity coach, and superconnector has said, *"You cannot have success without failure. The two are inextricably linked. So if you're afraid to act because you might make a mistake, stop and think again. Roadblocks and setbacks provide us with the information we need to grow, change and make a move in the right direction."*

When my son was five years old, all he wanted to be was a baseball player (just like me when I was his age) but as he grew older he finally found his real passion. In his sophomore year of high school he found music. He first learned how to play the guitar then moved on to the piano and then every instrument he could get his hands on. Finally, he ended up playing the tuba and it got him into a very prestigious college (the school of his dreams).

It wasn't until he got involved in Drum Corps International that his passion took off. He marched for three different Drum Corps and has toured all over the United States and has even played in front of 30,000 people. His passion is music but it doesn't stop there. His goal is to teach children how to play and to appreciate the gift of music. His passion will help him give back to others. His music isn't just a way to make a living but a way to make a life!

Passion is the force that drives our lives. If you have no passion you have no real purpose. That purpose brings happiness and that happiness leads to love.

God has given each one of us a special talent. Use it, develop it, and share it. Don't let anyone steal your dreams! If you don't succeed at first don't give up hope. It's not the end game but the journey that we find ourselves.

This quote from **Lao Zi**, the famous Chinese philosopher, sums up that journey: *"A journey of a thousand miles begins with a single step."*

Your journey in life begins with a single word… that word is **YES**? Follow your dreams and allow God to open up doors to bring you closer to him.

Following your passion can be emotionally challenging and with it comes a leap of faith, but don't worry about making the "wrong" choice because passion is just another word for love. Sharing your love with the world brings happiness to others.

Rupa Mehta, author of **"Connect To Your One"** and CEO of **NaliniKIDS** speaks of what passion really means: *"Sharing your passions is important to incorporating them into your everyday life but so is listening and asking others about their own. You never know what you'll learn about yourself when you ask someone else what they care about. Sharing and conversing about the most important parts of yourself with others can also strengthen your interpersonal relationships and thereby allow you to develop passions and interests outside of your comfort zone."*

Our passions can lead us to discovering many new friendships and ways to serve others. They make us whole and validate who we truly are. They give us an inner strength and a reason to be. **Rupa** goes on by saying, *"Passion is a powerful thing and by embracing, sharing and asking others about it we create a domino effect that could lead to a better and more open world. Be proud of who you are, what you're passionate about and share it."*

Finding our passion creates self-worth and that may be the greatest gift we can give ourselves.

What kind of person do you want to become? Do you have the direction you need to get there?

Best-selling author and screenwriter **Steven Pressfield** comments on what our mission is in life by stating: *"We come into this world with a specific, personal destiny. We have a job to do, a calling to enact, a self to become. Our job in this lifetime is not to shape ourselves into some ideal we imagine we ought to be, but to find out who we already are and become it."*

Your mission is to find your passion and through this passion live a life of love sharing your gifts with the world and filling your heart with the gifts of God. You don't have to be unhappy anymore, you don't have to feel like a loser as I used to feel, and you don't have to beat yourself up thinking you're not good enough. You are good enough and you will become the person you've always wanted to be. I believe in you and so does God!

That is something I wanted to hear all my life but never did until God spoke to my heart.

Passion is a zeal for life and with that passion you can accomplish great things. Passion is a way to become what you want while doing what you love. Without passion you are devoid of life. That was me for a long time. I wouldn't want to wish that kind of life on anyone, including you.

My passion is writing. I love to create. It is through this love that I hope to change lives. It is what makes me happy. Find what you are passionate about and you will find what makes you happy.

Bishop T. D. Jakes reminds us that *"If you can't figure out your purpose, figure out your passion. For your passion will lead you right into your purpose."*

Once you have your passion, you're on your way to becoming a more loving and caring person.

YOU WERE BORN FOR THIS

"God meets daily needs daily. Not weekly or annually.
He will give you what you need when it is needed."
—Max Lucado

Everyone goes through trials and tribulations. It's all part of life. The reason we are given these trials and tribulations is to prepare us for what our ultimate purpose is in life.

Everything you have experienced, everything you have learned, and everything you have been put through since you were born has been for a reason. God has given you the knowledge and the strength to live out your ultimate purpose. God does this to make you ready to handle the next phase of your life.

We may not like it nor do we enjoy the pain that comes with it but in order to equip us, **God** *"Works all things together for good to them that love God,"* as found in **Romans 8:28**. This divine purpose is *"To grow us more into the image of His Son,"* **Romans 8:29**.

Our trials are all part of the sanctification process which sets us aside for His Glory. *"In this you greatly rejoice, even though now for a little while, if necessary, you have been distressed by various trials, that the proof of your faith, being more precious than gold which perishes, even though tested by fire, may be found to result in praise and glory and honor at the revelation of Jesus Christ."* 1 Peter 1:6-7.

These trials and tribulations develop our character and help us rejoice in our sufferings because out of those sufferings comes perseverance, hope and endurance. God is perfecting us so that we can be mature in our love. He is molding us and shaping us to grow spiritually in His love.

Of course, we may not be able to see the wisdom of our trials but with faith we become stronger in knowledge and love of God. When you respond to these trials with God's grace, you will experience the healing power of God's Spirit.

How you respond to these trials makes all the difference. My whole life I ran away from my hardships instead of dealing with them head-on. I never fully realized that the problems I encountered were teaching me lessons about life. I had become a very bitter person but through God showing me his unconditional love, I saw a way out and transformed my life.

Today, I am fully dependant on God for all things. He has become my source of strength when I have none, provides for me when I cannot, and protects me when I am at my most vulnerable.

God has prepared you for your calling at this time. No matter how painful your past was, he has a calling for you. He puts people and situations in your life at the proper time in order to make you stronger.

There's another thing that God does for us that many people tend to forget. What we learn from our experiences we can use to help teach others and comfort them in their time of need. That is what I am doing now... using my experience and knowledge to help you when you need it.

Our walk with the Lord requires that we hope with faith, patience, and humility where we endure our sufferings to the end. Remember, nothing worth having ever comes easy or without some kind of opposition.

Our trials and tribulations are there to refine us and prepare us for a place that God has promised us. When we do the will of the Lord, nothing is wasted for His Glory.

The pain you felt from your previous experiences can be used to glorify God and bring you closer to Him. Use that pain as a stepping stone to living a life that truly matters.

DISCOVERING SELF-WORTH
FOR YOURSELF

*"Sometimes the hardest part of the journey
is believing you're worthy of the trip."*
—Glenn Beck

With passion comes a realization that you are somebody. This means you have self-worth. You can no longer feel apart from this world nor can you feel apart from God.

You must live your life by your own design. You are the one that counts. I've seen far too many people who live vicariously through others. They haven't developed their own personal likes or dislikes. They are like caricatures of others. These people have no sense of worth and try to lose themselves in the depths of society.

You are bigger than that. You are important! Don't let anyone tell you otherwise. Don't believe in your own limitations. God does not place limitations on you so why place them on yourself?

What kind of relationship are you having with life? Is the pain you feel inside banishing you from experiencing joy?

Louise L. Hay, the extraordinary author of **"You Can Heal Your Life"** and my personal hero states that, *"Your subconscious puts you where you are now. Your consciousness will either keep you there or lift you to a better position. It's up to you."*

Are you a victim of your own life? Are you willing to change and create your own destiny? I found this quote by an unnamed author really helps define who we are: *"You are wonderful. You are filled with wonder. You are the greatest mystery. Today, whatever you say will manifest and you will experience the wonder of you."*

Self-worth is defined as having a sense of one's own value or worth as a person. It should be less about measuring yourself against others and more about valuing your worth as a person. Don't judge yourself on what you've done but on who you are on the inside.

You have unique qualities that set you apart from others. These qualities are what define you as a person. The more you believe what others are saying or thinking about you instead of believing in yourself, the less self-worth you have.

This was my problem all along. I had no self-worth. I looked at myself and saw an ugly person who had no inherent qualities that made me unique. Even though I felt I could write, I subconsciously sabotaged everything I did so that I had a built-in excuse for failure. I realized I was afraid to succeed.

Dr. Lisa Firestone, a clinical psychologist and author of the book, **"Conquer Your Critical Inner Voice"** writes, *"We all have a "critical inner voice," which acts like a cruel coach inside our heads that tells us we are worthless or undeserving of happiness.*

She goes on to say, *"While these attitudes can be hurtful, over time, they have become engrained in us. As adults, we may fail to see them as an enemy, instead accepting their destructive point of view as our own."*

This critical inner voice is so destructive to our psyche. When we believe those nasty things about ourselves we end up having our biggest struggles in the area of relationships, financial troubles, stress, aggression and antisocial behavior.

Is this what has been keeping you from living the life you've always wanted to experience?

When you take the next step in your life things start to reveal themselves in a way that helps you manifest the best of the universe. Shift your thoughts and you shift your focus.

Discovering self-worth puts you on the path to finding love. It's a difference maker. I know. I am living proof of it!

What are you basing your self-worth on?

External factors seem to play a big part in how we define our self-worth. Things such as money, weight, and how people treat us can cause much internal strife. Add in physical, mental and emotional abuse and you can see how low self-worth can quickly turn into depression and anxiety.

If you struggle with low self-esteem like I did, you need to connect with others. Don't hide and wallow in self pity. Learn to celebrate the little victories in life. Search within yourself and figure out what it is you fear and look for ways you can find empowerment and strength in God.

Here is a biblical quote from **1 Samuel 16:7** that talks about self worth: *"But the Lord said to Samuel, Do not look on his appearance or on the height of his stature, because I have rejected him. For the Lord sees not as man sees: man looks on the outward appearance, but the Lord looks on the heart."*

We look to others to validate who we are but I've found that we need to validate ourselves first. I used to worry about what others thought about me, how they viewed me as a person, and what I looked like but now I've put the focus on others and it has made a world of difference in my own self-worth. It can make a world of difference to you also. The sky is the limit with you.

Ashley Fern, Director of Branded Social Strategy at **Elite Daily**, says self-respect is the key to self worth. *"This does not come easy so a conscious effort must be consistently made on a day-to-day basis. A lack of self-respect can, and most often does, result in depression and self-destructive behaviors. You need to reinforce your positive qualities and actively try to fix your negative qualities. When everything else in the world fails you, you will always have your self-respect to fall back on. How you feel about yourself affects every single aspect of your life."*

God wants you to see yourself the same way He see you. A person worthy of being loved and giving love to others in a way that benefits the entire world!

Now that you see yourself in a new way, we can now start to work on bringing more love into your life.

WHAT IS LOVE AND HOW
DO WE GET MORE OF IT?

"Keep love in your heart. A life without love
is like a sunless garden when the flowers are dead."
—Oscar Wilde

L OVE... it is a hypnotic word that has been overused to death. Everyone seems to talk about it though very few actually live a life based on love. It is in every song we sing, the movies show us their warped version of love (mostly sex) and books paint a picture of the virtues of love but how many of us actually practice what we preach?

Ask anyone and they will tell you they can't live without love but ask them if they are giving more than they take and you will hear excuse after excuse after excuse. So why is it that so many people cannot seem to get enough of it in their lives?

In fact, many people go through their entire lives without ever feeling the bonds of true love and this is a downright shame. We live in such an impersonal world where we hide behind things such as Facebook and Twitter that we don't even need human contact anymore to survive. Technology has become our surrogate parent and we are imprisoned by it.

Think I'm kidding?

Take a look what is happening to the young people of Japan. In an article taken from the Guardian Newspaper dated October 20, 2013, journalist **Abigail Haworth** wrote about how the youth of Japan (ages 18-40) are becoming virtual shut-ins and have an unhealthy aversion to all types of physical contact.

She writes, *"According to the government's population institute, women in their early 20's today have a one-in-four chance of never marrying. Their chances of remaining childless are even higher: almost 40% of Japan's under-40s appear to be losing interest in conventional relationships. Millions aren't even dating, and increasing numbers can't be bothered with sex. For their government, "celibacy syndrome" is part of a looming national catastrophe."*

The word love seems to have lost all meaning to them. This is happening all over the world. As economic times get tougher people seem to lose the meaning of what love actually is.

They become scared of love and what it entails. They are scared of opening up their hearts and taking a chance with love. The worst part is they have completely taken love out of their lives. These people have become so immersed in their own world that love isn't important anymore. The idea of caring for others and living a life where others are more important than themselves is now a foreign concept to them. People have become so selfish that they only care about their own distinct pleasure.

I decided to look up love in the dictionary (Merriam-Webster) and this is what I found:

1. strong affection for another arising out of kinship or personal ties *(2)*: attraction based on sexual desire: affection and tenderness felt by lovers *(3)*: affection based on admiration, benevolence, or common interests

2. an assurance of affection

3. warm attachment, enthusiasm, or devotion

4. the object of attachment, devotion, or admiration

5. a beloved person: darling - often used as a term of endearment

6. unselfish loyal and benevolent concern for the good of another: as (1): the fatherly concern of God for humankind (2): brotherly concern for others
7. a person's adoration of God
8. a god or personification of love
9. an amorous episode: love affair
10. the sexual embrace: copulation
11. a score of zero (as in tennis)

These definitions definitely miss the mark as to what love is and they certainly don't show us how to give or receive love.

I also looked up the definition of love in the Bible and it seems to gives us a better insight into what love is and how we should love but it doesn't explain why we are not living a life filled with love.

Here it is: **1 Corinthians 13:4-7**

Love is patient, love is kind. It does not envy, it does not boast, it is not proud. It does not dishonor others, it is not self-seeking, it is not easily angered, it keeps no record of wrongs. Love does not delight in evil but rejoices with the truth. It always protects, always trusts, always hopes, always perseveres.

I wanted to go deeper into the true meaning of love in this book and find a way that we can bring more love into this world as well as gratefully receive the love that is already here.

In the overall picture, love is something that's become a mystery to many people. They either equate it with sex or material objects but the underlying principal has been lost.

Don't believe me?

How many times have you said I love (insert object here). Whether it's pizza, football, romantic movies, cars… or whatever! You get the picture!

We're all guilty of this type of thinking but it can be changed and our happiness can be increased if we follow the powerful techniques I am about to share with you.

Have you ever asked yourself what is the true meaning of love?

You'd be surprised at how many people cannot answer this question. Love is a feeling for most people and they cannot put their finger on what love is all about.

Here is an example: Tell me how you feel after reading this next passage and be truthful. Have you ever felt this way?

Have you ever stepped back and watched an act of selfless love happen from a distance? How does it make you feel? Are you happy or sad? Does it spark feelings of jealousness or waves of thankfulness?

We are programmed by our nature to be selfish. It's who we are. Admit it, when you see someone else receiving love you get jealous. You don't initially feel happy for that person because you first look at your own life and if you are not receiving enough love then you become jealous of others.

How often do we give love to others without expecting anything in return?

No matter what the situation is, we as humans are always expecting something in return when we give. It makes us feel better about ourselves and fills a need. But what if you could change all that and see love in a whole new perspective?

Would you change how you love?

Would you change how you accept love?

What about how you give love?

The ideas in this book did not come easy to me. Definitely not! I've been through hell and back. I come from a broken and divorced home where we moved so many times during the first seven or eight years of my life and it took me ages to come to grips with my anger, my alienation from others, and my lack of trust.

Love is not something that just comes to us and we can handle it a responsible manner. It takes years of experience, unselfish attitudes, and a willingness to learn.

This book is not about what love is but how we can enjoy the love that is all around us and how we can freely give it back to others without expecting anything in return. On a deeper level, it is all about adding to our happiness and the happiness of those around us.

We are not islands unto ourselves but part of a bigger collective. As much as I am a true individual I couldn't make it in this world without others and neither can you.

When I was younger, I was a very negative person. I blamed others for my failures and I dwelled on my past defeats. I was a very unhappy person and it showed outwardly in my demeanor but more importantly, it was killing me emotionally.

I wanted love so badly. I needed love so much but nothing ever came my way. I was miserable but as I grew older I realized I needed to change my attitudes and the first thing that went was my selfishness.

Take it from me, it has been a long and painful journey but one that has taught me many lessons. Hopefully, you can see some parallels in your own life and take the necessary steps to increase the love you have.

In 1990, I met my future wife on a trip 10,000 miles from home. I didn't initially search for it but when it presented itself to me I grabbed it and held on tight. That may sound like a fairytale to you but there is all kinds of love everywhere… you just have to open yourself up and it let it appear. This, I can guarantee you 100%!

My wife is from the Philippines and together we have made a life for ourselves. It hasn't been easy but you "live and learn" as they say. We have three beautiful children who teach us about love on a daily basis and we are so proud of them.

I will be honest with you, finding love and giving love takes work. It takes a lot of time and it takes maximum effort. It's not something you can just snap your fingers and it instantly appears. On the other hand, the world is filled with so much love and you have to take the initiative and be willing to open your heart and grab it while you can.

Helping to bring more love into this world is a noble cause but one that many people will snicker at and call you self-righteous or even worse. They can't see it for what is really is. I'm not perfect and I don't expect you to be either. It's all about commitment to a higher principal.

The old line about *"It is better to give than receive"* is something we must all commit to. You will never find, keep, and give love if you don't make those words an important part of your life.

Whether you're a Christian, a Buddhist, a Muslim, Jewish, a believer or non-believer, love must be taken seriously. Without it, what is the use in living?

I don't profess to know everything about love… I just want to share it with others. Hopefully, you will take it seriously and try to make this world a better place for everyone around you.

If I can inspire more people to not only increase the amount of love in their lives but to give more love, then I believe I have done my job.

Each one of us has a job to do. We have been given a directive by God to love others as we would love ourselves. If you do this then you are discovering the true meaning of love.

We all know how much hate there is in this world and how much negativity and negative energy (whether purposely or done by accident) are being released, so it should come as no surprise that we all need to learn to accept love as well as give more of it.

But if you don't try, you won't find love.

The people you attract in your life are a reflection of who you are inside. You find others who are like you but if you don't take action to exercise your attraction genes then you miss opportunities to discover the greatness of others.

If you accept the differences between others and embrace what you have in common, you find the true meaning of love in the interaction. Sometimes, the forces of love are inspired by our own imagination. What we perceive to be love is just hope wrapped in a new blanket.

Love isn't something we need to think about. Instead, it is about living it in the moment. You can't feel love if you don't experience it!

THE MAIN ATTRIBUTES OF LOVE

"Let us always meet each other with a smile,
for the smile is the beginning of love"
—Mother Theresa

A s you can see, it is very hard to define love since most of us have a hard time inviting it into our lives. Love has its own set of unique attributes and knowing how to tap into these attributes will give us insight on what we need to do to be a more loving and caring person.

According to **Sarah Nean Bruce**, her poem called "**Love Versus Fear**" expresses the vast differences between love and fear. Fear of love is a very real fear in society. Fear of losing the love we have or even being rejected stops many people from taking the plunge.

If we can get a better understanding of what love consists of, maybe we won't be so afraid to love or even give love to others.

I've dissected this poem and compared the attributes of both and how they affect us.

LOVE VERSUS FEAR

1. **LOVE IS UNCONDITIONAL** - If we put restrictions on love then it really isn't love. Unconditional love is giving love without asking for anything in return and surrenders itself while fear forces us to accept obligations and binds us to its lies.

2. **LOVE IS STRONG** – Love endures through every pain, loss, and heartache but still remains while fear leaves at the very thought of weakness.

3. **LOVE IS HONEST** – Love is open and genuine and shows its integrity while fear is steeped in deceit and lies.

4. **LOVE GIVES** - Everything it has unselfishly while fear hides itself and resists all calls to be inclusive.

5. **LOVE IGNITES** – Our passions and embraces the desires of our heart while fear incites hate, anger, and disregards all that is good.

6. **LOVE CHOOSES TO FORGIVE** – With compassion and kindness while fear avoids blame, runs away, and is full of excuses.

7. **LOVE HEALS WITH MAGIC** – Which energizes the heart and allows inspiration to rule while fear is superstitious and tries to negate love with worry.

8. **LOVE IS AN ELIXIR THAT CREATES** - Sweet dreams filled with joy and abundance while fear saps our energy like a poison and needs to control our every action.

9. **LOVE RESPECTS** – By using patience and acceptance while fear uses pity and pressure to cause hurt and repudiation.

10. **LOVE IS BLIND** – In its belief and is brave enough to be free while fear is always afraid, always nervous, and full of judgment.

11. **LOVE IS FREE TO ENJOY** - Both in its beauty and affection while fear puts a price on all feelings and imprisons the heart with deception.

12. **LOVE BELIEVES** – That all things are possible and bears the brunt of every circumstance with trust while fear is always negative, always suffers, and rejects the needs of others.

H. Jackson Brown, Jr. once said that *"Love is when the other person's happiness is more important than your own."*

Regarding your own love, whose happiness is more important? Is it yours or the other person's? When you get that right, you will be on your way to knowing what real love is all about.

We celebrate love everyday but when we are in pain, our hearts are closed to the goodness of love. When you close it off, you cannot properly experience the true nature of love.

God is the epitome of love and all the attributes of love are God's attributes. When you accept that, you can freely enjoy the beauty of love.

Paul David Tripp is a pastor, author, and international conference speaker who published an article on February 10, 2015 entitled **"23 Things That Love Is"** which deeply touched my heart. Among the 23 things were two that I could really relate to because of all the pain I had encountered throughout my life.

1. Love is being willing, when confronted by another, to examine your heart rather than rising to your defense or shifting the focus.
2. Love is making a daily commitment to admit your sin, weakness, and failure and to resist the temptation to offer an excuse or shift the blame.

My entire life I couldn't come to grips with my sins, my weaknesses, and the hurt I felt when others pointed out my faults. I was defensive and I blamed everyone else for my own problems but God has invited me to be loved and has washed my sins clean. My heart is overflowing with his love and I wish to offer that love to you unconditionally.

I have learned so much from my past mistakes to be able to love again. The attributes that love entails are free to everyone. Remember, you are good enough to love and you are special enough to love. God loves you more than you could ever know.

STEP 1

FINDING LOVE'S
ULTIMATE POWER

OPEN YOUR HEART AND MIND
TO LOVE'S POSSIBILITIES

"I have decided to stick with love. Hate is too great a burden to bear."
—Martin Luther King, Jr.

L ove can be compared to a light bulb and you are the switch. In order to get the love flowing you must turn the switch on to the open position. When you open up your heart and your mind to all the possibilities of this world has to offer, you never know what can happen.

Love is power. The energy contained is very powerful indeed but when it's closed off it cannot work its magic. Yes, that's right... **Love IS Magic!**

What love does is very magical. It can turn the hardest of the hard into the sweetest of the sweet. On the other hand, a closed mind and a closed heart can do nothing. A closed mind gives nothing and receives nothing. It dies a lonely death without ever reaching its full potential.

I understand you've been hurt before. I get it! I've had so much heartache in my own life sometimes I wonder how I ever survived! When I was eighteen, the first real girlfriend I ever loved died of Leukemia. I was heartbroken. I couldn't believe how cruel love could be. Eventually, I came to grips with her loss but it left a big hole in my heart for a very, very long time.

The same thing goes for my family life. For many years, I believed I was cheated out of my childhood. Having a horrible family life, no friends, and feeling like I was a total loser really weighed heavily on my psyche. I've had confidence problems all my life. I never thought I was good enough for anyone or anything. It wasn't until I made the conscious decision to open up my heart and my mind to the possibilities that love offered did my life changed in dramatic fashion.

Heck, it was no fun being lonely, bored, and a complete failure but I came to grips with it all. Life is full of endless possibilities. You have to be a conduit for love.

What do I mean by that? Here is an analogy that I think sums it all up. If you are familiar with the Star Wars movies you'll see how this works.

In Star Wars, they talk of something called "**The Force.**" But exactly what is the Force? Well, it goes something like this:

In *Episode IV: A New Hope,* **Obi-Wan Kenobi** explains the idea of the Force to a young and very impressionable Luke Skywalker as *"An energy field created by all living things. It surrounds us, penetrates us, and binds the galaxy together."*

Those that are able to control it (like The Jedi) are conduits for its power. It took Luke many years but he was able to control the Force and become a Jedi Master. It was through his love of his father that he was able to save the galaxy from the evil Emperor Palpatine.

This sounds very much like love to me. Without love how could we all live? This force (love) is what binds us all together as the human race. The more love that is around, the less evil can wrangle its way into our lives. The more love we have the happier we will ultimately be.

Love is so powerful that it can ward off evil and fight the biggest of battles. Throughout the ages, people have done wondrous deeds in the name of love. On the other hand, some have used the excuse of love to conquer and hurt others. True love goes far beyond this.

Do you remember when you felt the grip of love for the first time? How did it make you feel inside? How was your demeanor to other people? Did the happiness you felt make everything in life that much sweeter? Would you like to experience that every day of your life? Would you like to help others experience that feeling also?

You can and I am going to show you how.

So then the next obvious question is: How do I open up my mind and my heart to bring more love into my life?

DOES IT REALLY MATTER WHAT'S INSIDE YOUR HEART AND MIND?

"Purity of speech, of the mind, of the senses, and of a compassionate heart are needed by one who desires to rise to the divine platform."

—Chanakya

You better believe it matters! It's how we all live! We are ruled by our emotions but we follow what's in our hearts and our minds to direct our actions.

Which one are you ruled by?

We've all heard the phrase **"Follow your heart"** but what does that actually mean? Have you ever allowed your heart to be ruled by your desires instead of what's logical?

Our desires can get us into real trouble if we're not careful. We can become easily confused if we're not able to use the principals of discernment.

I have made a ton of bad decisions over my lifetime. Many times I've let my hormones rule my judgment and have dated the wrong girl only to find out what a bad experience it was.

Other times, I didn't listen to my inner self and did things I shouldn't have done. My decisions caused me much pain but if I had listened to my intuition I would have avoided all the pain and heartache I caused myself.

Intuition is that little voice inside of us that tells us right from wrong. Desire is the competing voice telling us what feels better. It's kind of like having a good angel on one shoulder and a bad angel on the other arguing with you about what's right and what's wrong.

When we let emotions take over it changes how we treat others as well as how we think about ourselves. We become a different person. The kind of person who's heart and mind is blocked from receiving God's love.

In order for us to open ourselves up to receiving this love we need to change our thought patterns. God wants us to become a more loving person but in order to do this we have to take action.

Let's go through it one at a time so that you can understand how to open your heart and mind and then implement the ideas.

1. A blocked heart and a blocked mind are full of darkness and darkness leads to unhappiness.

    Martin Luther King Jr. once said, *"Darkness cannot drive out darkness: only light can do that. Hate cannot drive out darkness: only love can do that."* If you do not have an open mind and an open heart you allow so much pain to come in from things such as fear, hate, selfishness and negativity.

    The goal of love is to love unconditionally. Hence, if you live in darkness, you cannot see the love that is right in front of your eyes and you will miss those times when love is there to be seen, heard and felt.

2. A blocked heart and a blocked mind cannot grow. If you keep light from a plant, it will soon wither and die and so will you if you live in the clutches of darkness.

    Look, no matter what has happened before in your life, you need light to see. This light can guide you to where you are supposed to be and whom you are supposed to be with.

Are you ready to step out into the light? Yes, it may be hard and yes, there will be times when you're scared but you can't get anywhere if you don't take the first steps.

I have had co-workers who were so blind to life that all they ever saw was hatred and jealousy and were filled with worries and even rage. It is a sad thing to see. To waste your life with something that doesn't need to be yet here they were always focusing on the negative.

That brings us to the next point.

3. Let go of all your worries. If you are blocking love from coming out, these things will never disappear. You cannot change everything in life but you can change your own thoughts, your own feelings, and your own bad habits.

    "But it's so hard to do," I hear people complain about this all the time. Of course it's hard but that doesn't mean it cannot be done. Too much worry puts the emphasis on ourselves instead of God working in us. Remember, we have free will and when we cut God out of that will we are prone to worrying about things we have no control over. When you worry, you close yourself off to opportunities to experience the joys that God has planned for you.

4. A blocked heart and a blocked mind limit your choices in life. What could be worse than having no choices at all? When you limit your choices you limit the possibilities that life brings.

    When I was young, I wanted to be a writer but things always got in the way. I gave myself lame excuses as to why I couldn't start working on my dreams and so it limited my choices for happiness and I suffered greatly for it.

    I would complain all the time and never got out of my doldrums. I'd wonder to myself if I was ever going to fulfill my dreams or get stuck in a forty hour workweek with no time, no money, and no hope.

    I had this voice deep inside of me crying out for years and years until I opened up my heart and my mind to the endless possibilities if I just gave God's love a fleeting chance.

    Gradually, one thing led to another and I started meeting the right people who cared about me. Doors opened and I took advantage of them. No more lack of confidence, no more excuses, and no more unhappiness. I fulfilled my dreams and became a published author. Of course, it took a lot of work and I went into deep debt to get there but I remained open to the love of others who guided me and appreciated my talents.

The change in my heart was the key to what I've become in my new life. I never knew what I could accomplish until I gave love a chance to grow. The power of love transcends all time and space. It was always there but I never knew how to access it. My mind was still limited to what I felt or saw and I didn't allow the magic of love to work in my life.

These experiences are not limited to just me. Many people I know had trouble overcoming abandonment, feeling unloved and uncared for until they were able to bring the power of love into their life.

For me, the car accident was the impetus for my own change of heart. It was a choice I will never regret!

Saint Thérèse de Lisieux once said we should, *"Miss no single opportunity of making some small sacrifice, here by a smiling look, there by a kindly word; always doing the smallest right and doing it all for love."*

Every small sacrifice is a chance to bring more love into the world. What you do for others, your Father in heaven sees. Do it all for the sake of love and you'll see how your blessings will be multiplied and given back to you with unconditional love.

LIVING WITH YOUR CHOICES

"When you wake up every day, you have two choices. You can either be positive or negative; an optimist or a pessimist. I choose to be an optimist. It's all a matter of perspective."
—Harvey Mackay

We all have choices to make in life and no one is immune from the consequences of those choices. The problem is our inability to learn and go forward from our past mistakes. Like me, many of you are both too stubborn and too unwilling to change who you are that you end up living a life less than what you envisioned.

Let me tell you this… my stubbornness got me into a lot of trouble. I thought I was living a righteous life but I was unwilling to change my thinking because I was fearful of change! Fear is what stops many of us from implementing the changes we need to live a life based on love.

I was so paralyzed with fear about making the wrong choices that I did nothing at all. I lost sight of what it was I wanted to do with my life and how I was supposed to act. This is one of the main reasons I kept failing at everything.

From music (none of the bands I was in ever accomplished anything even though I was writing songs all the time), to work (I was always stuck in what I felt were dead-end jobs that didn't use my God-given talents), to relationships (I was so fearful of rejection that I rejected myself before others did), to business (I never put any of the information I learned into concrete action and my businesses all failed leaving me deep in debt).

I know what some of you may be thinking. *"You don't know my situation."* Or *"Life's been cruel to me."* Or even *"I'm just an unlucky person."* Those are just lame excuses. Believe me, I know. I've used every excuse in the book.

Look, I get it. I really do but unless you are willing to change your thinking and start taking responsibility for the choices you have made in life then you are going to be stuck in the same place you've always been... sick and tired of feeling unloved, unappreciated, unhappy and going through life lost and angry at everyone and everything.

You want to change your life but like me, fear is your worst enemy. You need to understand what choices you've made in the past and how to go beyond those mistakes and start designing a new future that is both bright and full of love.

You are a reflection of the choices you make whether good or bad. We are not immune to problems in our lives but when we choose to deal with these problems in a mature and logical way we can overcome them.

Life is really one big test after another. How you choose to deal with these problems is what sets happy and successful people apart from unhappy and unsuccessful people. It really doesn't matter how much chaos you have going on in your life (we all lead crazy lives), it's about how well you manage the chaos.

Listen, nothing is easy in life but you have to open both your hearts and your minds to see what lies before you. You cannot look back because you cannot change the past. You can only change the present.

When people are unhappy, they tend to blame everything else but themselves. They sabotage their lives thinking they will always be broke, always be unhappy, and always be unlucky.

What you need to understand, what I have finally understood, is that you match what you believe with who you are, because our choices are a reflection of our personalities.

Let's go over what you can do to make better choices so it puts you in a position to bring more love into your lives.

1. **Be humble** - The journey towards making better decisions begins with humbling yourself before God and letting him show you what choices you need to make. As humans, most of our decisions are made by pure emotion and that is where we go wrong. Research has shown that humans make decisions 10 seconds before they are consciously aware of it.

    Seek wisdom, pray for integrity in your dealings, and commit yourself to a higher calling. Love is not something you take as if it were an object. Love is something that comes to those who open their hearts to it.

2. **Does the decision benefit everyone involved?** - Remember, it's not always about you. There are others involved in your life and it will affect them also.

    When I decided to become an author, I had to make some important decisions regarding how much time to allot to my writing, such as when I could write and where I could write because I had three young children at the time that needed me to be there for them. I couldn't just set my own rules without taking their needs into consideration. What you do does affect others. Make your decisions based on others needs and you will make better decisions.

3. **Base you choices on sound moral principles** - We get into trouble when the choices we make don't jive with what is morally right. Keep a balanced approach to your decisions by making choices based on who you are and what you believe in so that you don't follow down a path of pain and misery.

4. **Look for opportunities to grow** - Sometimes we have to make tough choices that will help us later on. Not all decisions are easy and there are no guarantees in life but if you think of this as a test and you fail, it's not the end of the world. Many times I thought I made the wrong decision but ended up realizing my mistakes taught me some valuable lessons about life. All you can do is your best, that's what life asks of you.

5. Be **wary of basing your choices on just your heart.** - The difference between instinct and desire is a big one. Quick decisions are usually

done with desire while well thought out decisions require a balance between instinct and logic.

So why are my choices so important to love?

Every day we have to make choices whether we want to or not. Your choices determine how you will love and be loved in return.

Don't believe me?

How you treat others is all about making the right choices. Make a bad choice and you could lose the friendship of someone you really care about. Make the right choice and people will treat you with care and respect.

Isn't that the way you want to be treated? Of course it is but all of us have horror stories of being mistreated. It's all part of life. You can't let those things bother you.

You have the power to make your own choices. No one holds that power over you. The most important thing to remember when making your choices is **"what are the consequences of that decision?"** Follow this and everything you do will have a logical conclusion to your answer.

In her book, **"The Pursuit of Happiness: 21 Spiritual Rules to Success,"** **Jennifer O'Neill** shines a light on why our thinking needs to change if we are to make better choices. *"You are never stuck, unless you are choosing to stay there. You are never limited, unless you choose to limit yourself. You are never less than, unless you choose to see yourself this way. You will never fail, unless you choose failure as an option. You are powerful beyond belief!"*

Do you want to settle for anything but success in your life? Don't choose the idea that you have no other choice but to fail. Don't be the victim. Instead, make wise choices that align with what you believe and how you want to see your future self.

Are you making choices that move your life forward? If not, then those choices are keeping you stuck in your current situation. Your happiness depends on you, not other people. Make your choices based on what is good for you not what other people want you to do and happiness will then follow.

You will avoid untold pain and regret if you make your decisions based on instant gratification. Follow your decisions to their logical end before you decide so you have the outcome in hand before you make the commitment.

LIVING WITH YOUR FEARS

*"Living with fear stops us taking risks, and if you don't
go out on the branch, you're never going to get the best fruit."*
—Sarah Parish

There are two motivating forces in life: One is fear and the other is love. With love, we have the opportunity to create a life filled with beauty and passion. It is our natural state of grace. On the other hand, when we are afraid, we pull ourselves away from life. We accept negativity, judgment, sadness, and depression and give into our own worst emotions.

Fear is something all of us encounter but it can take over our entire lives. With fear, we tend to see ourselves differently than how others see us and we fear the worst in ourselves. When we don't think high enough of ourselves, fear becomes our driving force.

To live in love is to find your true place in this world. It is where your passion and your purpose come together. Fear paralyzes that love and suffocates your creativity. Fear is what holds you back from being what God intended you to be.

Love and fear cannot exist together. We as humans choose fear because we are afraid of love. It's plain and simple. Fear stops us from allowing love to bring peace and happiness into our lives. When we are in a state of fear, our hearts cannot access the power to love.

Those that act out of fear, act in selfish disregard of how others feel by inspiring more fear. Instead, love is who we are. It is given to us from the **ONE** who created us and it is how we are to live.

From **1 John 4:18,** the bible has a beautiful quote that puts love and fear into context and shows us why we shouldn't fear love at all. *"There is no fear in love: true love has no room for fear, because where fear is, there is pain; and he who is not free from fear is not complete in love."*

Fear directs our attention away from a life of love and blinds us to the realities of life. We let fear dictate how we feel and this smothers any love we might have.

In high school, I was a very shy person. Sports and music were basically my life. I hid myself away from everyone and lived vicariously through my music and my writings. Although I loved to write, it didn't take the place of real experience. I missed the experience of communicating with others because of fear. It took me so long to come out of my shell and feel the love of others. Without love I existed instead of living.

For many years I was so jealous of others when I saw them performing on stage. I knew in my heart I could do it but my fear of failure was too much to handle. It stopped me from truly experiencing the things that made me happy.

Even to this day, I have trouble overcoming self-doubt but I don't give in to my fears. I have learned that if you want something bad enough you have to fight for it. That means looking fear in the eye and saying **"You will not stop me!"**

How much more love can you express when you see what love can do? Loved changed my life and it can change yours.

Love is all within us. It's not an illusion. It is not a game. It is all in how we choose to see love. Whether we say yes or say no, our choices define how we react to love. Fear has no place in love.

Freelance writer, **Nadia Ballas-Ruta** writes, *"Perception of a situation determines our thoughts and that in turn creates how we feel about a situation. Thoughts and feelings work hand in hand. Each one influences the other."*

Our fears are all based on phony perceptions that cause us to devalue ourselves. It is so easy to see but hard to change. What prevents us from taking the risk is the outcome which is not guaranteed.

But that's the beauty of life. Nothing is guaranteed but you have to be committed to taking action and making your dreams come true. If you sit on the sidelines you will never get into the game. The idea is to get in the game and play. Make things happen. You will fail at times but more often than not, you will succeed. That's how to overcome your fears.

William Shakespeare once wrote that *"Life is a stage and we each must play a part."* Don't be the audience and watch your life from the cheap seats. Don't let fear intimidate you. Your message of love will shine through when you take action.

Here Are Four Ways You Can Overcome Your Fears

1. **Analyze your fears** - Find out what triggers them so you can decide what you need to do to deal with the problem. Follow a plan to logically build up your confidence to deal with your own anxieties and limitations and then determine the consequences of your fears.

2. **Change your thoughts about what fear really is** - When you see fear as just an emotion and not based in reality then you can summon the courage to directly confront fear for what it is. Plan ahead for possible scenarios where you can deal with the consequences in a rational and proactive way.

3. **Make fear an opportunity for real change in your life** - Use it to prepare yourself because knowledge is power when conquering your fears. When you learn why you are fearful you can break it down into smaller pieces where you can understand why your fear sabotages you.

4. **Take control of your fears by getting control of your imagination** - Change your perception by shrinking the fears in your mind until they stop diminishing your determination.

Remember, what's the worst that can happen to you? You might fail… Big deal! Everyone fails even successful people like Albert Einstein, Michael Jordan, and Bill Gates. Failure is just another word for experiencing life.

I was once frozen with fear getting interviewed on the radio. I thought I would forget what I wanted to say. I would stutter, or even say the wrong things but after doing over 150 interviews I still get the butterflies in my stomach but the fear is gone. Why? Because I confronted it and did not let that little voice inside my head talk me out of doing what I wanted to do.

FOCUSING ON LOVE

*"We experience God to the extent to which we love,
forgive, and focus on the good in others and ourselves."*
—Marianne Williamson

W hen you focus on the things you want, you consciously manifest those things in your life. How you direct your thoughts links you to those actions. Continue with fear and you create your own circumstances. Those circumstances impact how you love others.

What are you focusing on?

If fear is your focus others will see it in your words and actions. Empower the love you have within you and direct those thoughts so that you can transform your outcomes. When you combine love with positive action you will prosper.

Pain causes us to turn away from love and focus on the negative aspects of life. When you focus on love, you will attract love to yourself. God's unconditional love eases your pain and focuses your heart on what is really important – giving and sharing love with others.

Rick Warren, the well-known pastor and bestselling-author of **"A Purpose Driven Life"** says that *"You don't know God is all you need until God is all you've got. But that's all you need, because God will take care of you."*

It's true. God's love will always be there for you and when you share that love and focus it on others you will see a huge change in your own life.

Focus brings clarity and clarity brings lucidity to every situation. We learn how to love when we can clearly focus on the serenity of love.

My problem all those years was not being clear about who I was and what I wanted out of life. It always started and ended with me. I admit it... I was selfish. At the time I felt alone and scared but it was because I didn't focus my attention on love.

Clarity also brings abundance. This abundance is not a material thing but a spiritual awakening. It comes with an abundance of love that we need to share. When we respond to others with kindness and love, we can change someone's world.

It only takes one person's world to make a difference. Focus on one person at one time and make it count. Your love may be exactly what that person needs right now. Be an instrument of love that manifest's its abundance on others. Create a passion for love that you can then focus on others.

I felt that love and it saved my life. Each person I meet I try to focus on being that one person they can trust. ... that one person they can feel at ease with... that one person who inspires them with unconditional love.

We have a responsibility to focus our love where it does the most good. In **Colossians 3:9-10**, the **Apostle Paul** tells us, *"You have taken off your old self with its practices and have put on the new self, which is being renewed in knowledge in the image of its Creator."*

As I grew in love, my old habits died and my new character took on imitating Christ. I'm not perfect but as I focus on loving others, I find a certain amount of happiness rich in sweetness which comes from loving others. It is a joy that cannot be expressed with mere words but with unselfish actions.

Those that excel at loving others focus on the things that matter the most such as a person's heart and character. Who we are inside is what Christ focuses on so shouldn't we do the same?

Tony Robbins, the world famous Self-Help guru states that we need to shift our focus to bring about lasting change. *"Where focus goes, energy flows. And where energy flows, whatever you're focusing on grows. In other words, your* *life is controlled by what you focus on. That's why you need to focus on where you want to go, not on what you fear. When you next find yourself in a state of uncertainty, resist your fear. Shift your focus toward where you want to go and your actions will take you in that direction."*

What we do in life is a true expression of the love we have inside. If we focus on those things that give love, we bring happiness to both ourselves and others but if we focus our energies on things that don't involve love, we end up wasting our time and effort on things that never work.

People resist change and try the same things over and over again hoping for different results. You have to change what you do and model yourself after Jesus. His way gets results. Our ways are crude and haphazard.

According to **Isaiah 55:8**, *"For My thoughts are not your thoughts, Nor are your ways My ways, declares the LORD."*

Live by God's ways and you will find more love than you could ever know.

The key to focusing on love is to have a model you can imitate. Jesus is that model. When you imitate his love with other people you bring out the best in everyone.

CAN YOU FIND HAPPINESS
WITHOUT LOVE?

"Affection is responsible for nine-tenths of whatever
solid and durable happiness there is our lives."
—C. S. Lewis

Have you ever met someone who loved life without being happy?
Of course not but the majority of people base their entire lives on the amount of possessions they have and when they die they realize it was all a waste of time. Love is something we can take anywhere we go, with anyone we want, and at anytime we choose. Without love there would be no happiness to speak of.

When there was no love in my life I was very unhappy, yet the minute love entered, happiness came along for the ride. We think that money, fame, and possessions can bring us all the happiness we ever want but without love it makes everything else useless.

Looking back over my life, the times I was happiest were the times when there was a deep sense of feeling loved that went along with it. The times when my life was devoid of love were the hardest for me to take. There was loneliness, rejection, and anger all rolled into one.

Finding true happiness starts and ends with love. Our purpose in life is to love and to be happy. The great poet, **Oliver Wendell Holmes Sr.** wrote this about love and happiness, **"Love is the master key that opens the gates of happiness"**.

We are all here because of God's unconditional love and we are forgiven because of his love. His master key opens the door to happiness and we feel God in all his wonderful love. When we go looking for happiness, we think and hope we'll find it but when we don't, we are devastated to the core!

According to **Thich Nhat Hanh**, a Vietnamese Buddhist monk and peace activist, *"True happiness should be based on peace."* And later he says, *"Therefore, if you don't have peace in yourself you have not experienced true happiness."*

Where does that peace come from? It comes from purifying your mind and focusing on the love of God. It comes from the trust your life matters to God and that He has a purpose for it. Too often we search our entire lives for happiness yet it is right there in front of our eyes.

What Is The Real Meaning Of Happiness?

Happiness can be looked upon as a journey. A journey that we start with the Lord by your side and then continues throughout your life. It is through Him that we see the beauty that surrounds us. But happiness does not bring forth love. Love is an action which brings forth happiness into our lives.

When you make the choice to show love you bring a bit of happiness into the world. This is why it's so puzzling to me when people decide to hide themselves away from life. There is no love and no happiness in being alone… only pain and isolation. I know… I've been there and done that and it doesn't work!

Happiness is something we choose from the inside of our hearts. By approaching each new situation with love, we create our own brand of happiness. This brand of happiness requires a certain risk on our part… a risk most of us do not want to take. But true happiness always requires some type of struggle if we are to find love.

God wants us to learn how to love like he does. He wants us to give love like he does and that can be a huge struggle for most people. That struggle is what shapes us and molds us into the people we eventually become. Happiness flows from our hearts when we choose to love. Nowhere else can we find as much happiness as we do when we love others like we do God.

In 2012, Harvard psychiatrist **George Vaillant** released the findings of a seventy-five year study done at Harvard which studied the intimate lives of 268 men in a book entitled **"Triumphs of Experience: The Men of the Harvard Grant Study"**. In it, they found you cannot underestimate the power of love because it's the key to happiness.

Dr. Vaillant e stated, *"Happiness is love. Full stop! The journey from immaturity to maturity is a sort of movement from narcissism to connection, and a big part of this shift has to do with the way we deal with challenges.*

We all have challenges in life but God is there working on us, helping us to become the person we were meant to be, and our happiness is in the appreciation of everyday things, not just the extraordinary.

Most happiness is superficial and does not last long enough to bring any type of peace into our lives. That type of happiness is transitory and constantly needs to be updated or we fall into depression. A great example of this is when we receive presents during the holiday. We get excited at first but then we go looking for the next fix. You cannot do that because it just doesn't work. You need a solid foundation with love as the anchor and from there happiness will flow from appreciating everything that comes your way.

Happiness and love go hand in hand yet we seek only one at a time. Seek the love of God and happiness follows.

God has called us to be great ambassadors of love. It is your job as a Christian and one you shouldn't take lightly.

FORGIVE, FORGET
AND MOVE FORWARD

*"The weak can never forgive. Forgiveness
is the attribute of the strong."*
—Mahatma Gandhi

T he one thing that stops most people from experiencing true love and giving of one's self is not learning how to forgive others. Mother Theresa once said, "If we really want to love, we must learn how to forgive."

Forgiveness takes a huge burden off of our minds and allows us to go forward. When we don't forgive, we stay stuck in the past and don't allow ourselves to appreciate what came before.

If you have been hurt or betrayed and you can't find a way to begin the forgiveness process then healing cannot begin. This healing is not only emotional but a physical one as well.

Studies have shown that the resentment that comes from not forgiving your past can lead to heart disease, a weakened immune system as well as various forms of cancer. When you let go of old grudges and the anger associated with them you are able to reduce your stress levels, your anxiety will decrease, and you can avoid depression. This healing is the first stage of a greater psychological well-being.

According to the Mayo Clinic, forgiveness leads to:

1. Healthier relationships
2. Greater spiritual and psychological well-being
3. Less anxiety, stress and hostility
4. Lower blood pressure
5. Fewer symptoms of depression
6. Stronger immune system
7. Improved heart health
8. Higher self-esteem

Remember, you forgive others not just for them but for yourself as well. Do it for your own piece of mind. The harder it is to let go of the anger, the harder you will make it on yourself to be happy. When you are able to let go of those hateful feelings, you break free of its bonds. The more you hold on, the more it becomes your fault. Forgive yourself and it will become easier to forgive others.

In his book, **"Your Best Life Now: 7 Steps to Living at Your Full Potential"**, **Pastor Joel Osteen** describes what happens to people who haven't been able to forgive and have let their anger take over their hearts. *"Keep in mind, hurting people often hurt other people as a result of their own pain. If somebody is rude and inconsiderate, you can almost be certain that they have some unresolved issues inside. They have some major problems, anger, resentment, or some heartache they are trying to cope with or overcome. The last thing they need is for you to make matters worse by responding angrily."*

For years, I felt so much anger to all of those people who hurt me while I was still in school. This unresolved anger was taken out on everyone I came in contact with and I didn't realize I was doing it. Kids can be very cruel and they made me feel like such an outsider when I was young but now I look upon it as a growth experience because it helped toughen me up.

I kept those feelings in the dark recesses of my soul and just couldn't forgive any of them no matter how hard I tried but I realized they made me who I am today; A strong individual who has so much love to offer and so many rich experiences to draw upon whenever I write.

SHEDDING GUILT FROM YOUR HEART

*"Guilt is cancer. Guilt will confine you, torture you,
and destroy you as an artist. It's a black wall. It's a thief."*
—Dave Grohl

The object of guilt causes so much unnecessary pain in our lives. We harbor ill will for others when they hurt us but nothing is as deep or as penetrating as living with your own guilt. It is a self-destructive attitude that sabotages your entire life.

I wrestled with my own guilt for years. I used to think my problems were all my fault and I would often beat myself up over every misstep I made. If I said the wrong thing at the wrong time to someone or didn't do as well as I should have on a test or even playing sports at school then I would heap all kinds of guilt upon my shoulders.

I put too much pressure on myself to do well because of my self-esteem problems. I felt I had to do better than everyone else just to fit in. I had this poor self-image and it ruined my life. It was like I was chained to a pole and life was slapping me silly!

So what changed me?

Love… a simple four letter word. When I changed my toxic attitudes my life began to change. When I stopped beating myself up and accepted my faults, the stress diminished and I was able to come to terms with my pent-up guilt.

Guilt tears us down and makes us feel unworthy. It is our conscience alerting us that what we are about to do goes against our values. But at its very core, guilt keeps others in control.

Guilt is cultivated when we allow ourselves to dwell on our past failures and doesn't give healing a chance to work in our hearts and minds. We continually struggle with a problem that has no solution. Once we let it fester it's like a cancer that has no cure. **Mahatma Gandhi** once said, *"I will not let anyone walk through my mind with their dirty feet."*

We need to learn how to take our thoughts captive and trust in a higher power. This is where faith comes in. Faith crushes guilt by the very fact that **Jesus** gives us the peace to go on. **Romans 5:1** tells us this; *"Therefore, since we have been justified by faith, we have peace with God through our Lord Jesus Christ."*

Without faith, you are left to your own devices to deal with these feelings but through faith we have been forgiven and have the power to go on.

There are two types of guilt that we suffer from.

1. **Guilt as a stimulant for inner change** - Healthy guilt is used to stimulate change in our lives. It helps protect us from overstepping the boundaries of our core values and beliefs. Learning from our past mistakes helps us mature and take responsibility for our actions.

2. **Guilt as a tormentor** – Is based on false expectations we have of ourselves that we can never live up to. It imprisons us by controlling our thoughts, feelings, and actions. It impedes our normal way of life and keeps up locked in the past.

Why Is Guilt So Powerful And How Can You Free Yourself Of The Guilt?

1. **Recognize your guilt – Understand the type of guilt you are suffering from and its main purpose in your life. Once you recognize the type of guilt you have, you can tackle it at its inner core.**

2. **Accept that you did something wrong but move on** - We all make mistakes so don't try to be perfect. Just be yourself.
3. **Start learning from your behaviors** - Every time you make a mistake, learn from it so the next time you can avoid those guilty feelings. It's all part of the maturity process.
4. **Implement changes now rather than later** - The quicker you enact changes the quicker they become good habits. Concentrate on changes that are good for you rather than change for change sake.
5. **Perfection does not exist** - the quicker you realize that the quicker you can move on with your life. Don't try to be perfect all the time. Live life and enjoy it. Don't take the good out of life if you happen to make a mistake. Just know it is all part of growing and learning.

Guilt affects all parts of our life… from emotional to physical to spiritual and if it is allowed to fester it can lead to unhealthy attitudes. Carrying the burden of guilt stops love from healing the pain we have our hearts. Let God heal your guilt and give you strength to live a life filled with unending love.

HOW CAN I FORGIVE OTHERS?

"Forgiveness is the final form of love."
—Reinhold Niebuhr

Forgiveness is a very personal and complex path that has different stages for each person involved. It's one of life's greatest challenges. In order to forgive you must acknowledge that you are part of the event that has happened. Don't deny the event ever happened or that you played a part in it. No matter who is to blame, committing yourself to choosing forgiveness is your first step.

If you can resist the temptation to dwell on the anger you have and look beyond the hurt, you can then give absolution to those that have hurt you. When you can move on from those toxic emotions that suppress your natural feelings of gratitude and love, happiness is the end result. And who doesn't want to be happy?

What if you cannot forgive others?

You have to understand, there's no benefit in keeping that anger inside. When you don't forgive, it can "eat you up." It is a self-inflicted punishment that you can overcome but you have to really want it.

That was a hard lesson I had to learn. Each day, I let my anger boil up inside until one day it burst and I regretted what I did. Don't let it go that far. Every steam pot needs a vent. Find that vent and allow your anger to diminish. This is your first step towards forgiveness.

According to **Frederic Luskin, PhD**, director of the Stanford University Forgiveness Project says that, *"You can't just will forgiveness."* **Dr. Luskin**, who is also the author of "**Forgive For Good: A Proven Prescription for Health and Happiness**," states that, *"You can create conditions where forgiveness is more likely to occur. There are specific practices that diminish hostility and self-pity, and increase positive emotions, so it becomes more likely that a genuine, heartfelt release of resentment will occur."*

That heartfelt release is the love we are looking for. Those positive emotions will come bubbling up and help you define your feelings from that moment on.

Here Are 7 Ways To Reduce Anger And Allow Yourself The Chance To Forgive

1. **Pray for the other person** - When someone hurts you, pray that they will find their way back to a place of happiness. Love the sinner not the sin. Love them for who they are not what they have done to you.

2. **Count your blessings** - No matter what happens to us, we should be thankful for what we have. Life has a way of sending problems our way as a test of our character. What are you lacking? Is it patience? Compassion? Resilience? Or just plain forgiveness? One way or another the test will come. Will you be ready for it?

3. **Think about a time when you were forgiven and how that felt to you** - Use those feelings to send forgiveness back to those that need it. Allow forgiveness to lift the burden of hate and bring calmness to your soul.

4. **Face your anger head on** - Don't avoid dealing with it. It will only spiral off into more hurt and more anger. Instead, face what is bothering you.

   Robert Enright, PhD, a professor of educational psychology at the University of Wisconsin-Madison, co-founder of the **International Forgiveness Institute** and author of *"Forgiveness Is a Choice" says: "Forgiveness should be a joyous gift, not a grim obligation. If you* *try to force it, you'll just end up feeling pressured and perhaps guilty if you're unable to follow through. Set your intention to forgive, and then do it at your own pace, knowing it might take days, weeks or months."*

5. **Forgiveness is a process that takes time** - *It doesn't mean you have to lose all of those feelings. It just doesn't* take center stage in your heart anymore. Make peace with your pain. That is the difference between conquering your pain and succumbing to it.

6. **Be transformed by your forgiveness - Michael Hidalgo**, a pastor at Denver Community Church and the author of "**UnLost: Being Found by the One We Are Looking For**" says this about forgiveness. *"It's not that we dismiss the pain, or discount the difficulty of our journey. But it does mean we recognize that even our greatest wounds, deepest pain and greatest agony will one day be transformed into beauty by the God who wastes nothing."*

   The act of total forgiveness can be found on the cross. It is from there that we take our cue. **Pastor Michael** continues, *"In the cross, we see the memory of our sin placed squarely on the person of God who removes our sin and the memory of pain. It's as though God Himself says, "I'll take your hurt - all of it - even the painful memories. This is what I did when I died for you."*

7. **Verbally forgive** - I have used this technique to help me overcome many of my own feelings of anger. I made a huge commitment to make peace with those who hurt me. By looking in the mirror and verbally forgiving my tormentors, I found it liberating to feel all that hate and anger just fall off my shoulders as if it never was there at all. But remember, once you have verbally forgiven in this manner, you must take the next step. Going face to face and forgiving in person.

Forgiveness is hard. We all know that but we have a great teacher in Jesus who has forgiven us of our sins. This is why we need to follow His example. When we do, the idea of forgiveness becomes something we can live with despite the anger and pain.

We all have our own cross to bear but it becomes much lighter when God is holding it with us.

WHAT EFFECT DOES HOLDING A GRUDGE HAVE ON A PERSON?

"Carrying a grudge is a heavy burden. As you forgive,
you will feel the joy of being forgiven."
—Henry B. Eyring

Disguised as anger, grudges are like a volatile poison that grabs hold of you and slowly sends you spiraling out of control. The effects are mind-numbing when you think about it. It can cause deep-seeded emotional barriers between people and families that can last a lifetime.

I have seen families that haven't talked to each other in years because one person is still holding a grudge against the other and everyone else is paying the price for it. It may sound ridiculous (and it is) but when emotions are enflamed anything is possible.

Here Are Just Some Of The Effects To
Look Out For When Holding A Grudge

1. Grudges bring negative emotions based on anger, bitterness, and resentment into every relationship and new experience. You could be pushing others away and not even know it by your own negative actions.

2. Holding a grudge forces you to become so wrapped up in the hate inside you that you can't enjoy what's happening here in the present.

3. Holding a grudge feeds your depression and anxiety and easily takes over your life making it harder to do anything at all.

4. You may feel your present life lacks any type of meaning or purpose and you give into your feelings of hopelessness.

5. You lose the closeness that comes with experiencing life with others and you become more of a loner.

Remember the line, **"To err is human, to forgive is divine."** It is a powerful reminder that forgiveness begins and ends with you. You are responsible for forgiving others. You cannot change them, only yourself.

Here Are 5 Questions To Help Rid Yourself Of The Anger, Hate and Rage You May Still Feel Inside

1. What is it that makes me feel this way?

2. Can I change the past or am I clinging to a moment in time that I don't want to lose?

3. Am I scared of changing my ways?

4. Will I be hurt again?

5. Is my health suffering because of the undo pressure I'm putting on myself?

If you're looking to end the grudges you feel are holding you back, counter the negative by using a positive. Let go of your attachments to how you think things should be or how you think others should be acting. This means, use the encounter as a life lesson and go on from there. You will be much happier for it and it will save you heartache in the future.

Dealing with grudges keeps you locked in time. It is as if you stopped living from that point on with the other person. I understand all the anger and rage you are feeling but it almost ruined my life. I leave it all up to Jesus now. I let Him take care of the problem. I'm not strong enough nor wise enough to do it myself.

God wants you to surrender your problems, your thoughts, and most especially your heart to Him so that He can change you into the person He wants you to be. That is the biggest obstacle I had to overcome but once I did, life became much sweeter as a result.

WHAT HAPPENS IF I CAN'T FORGIVE?

*"He that cannot forgive others, breaks the bridge over
which he himself must pass if he would ever reach
heaven; for everyone has need to be forgiven."*
—George Herbert

F orgiveness is a challenging subject, especially if the subject to
which you cannot forgive is not around anymore or refuses to
acknowledge you.

Everyone needs to be forgiven but those that refuse it cannot look
backwards and have no way to move forward. You, on the other hand
must do everything in your power to see things from a different point
of view. Without it, your pathway is clouded by your own emotional
judgments.

Here Are 5 Things You Can Do Right Now To Understand Your Situation More Clearly

1. Have you ever considered the situation from the other person's point of view? Put yourself in their shoes and try to understand why they did what they did.

2. Would you have acted the same way? Maybe you would have reacted similarly if you knew what the other person was going through.

3. Remember, there were times in your life when you've hurt others and they have forgiven you. Everyone has been hurt at one time or another so try to understand that you share in the guilt of pain and you need to acknowledge your role in hurting others so that you can forgive both yourself and others for what has transpired in the past.

   In **Matthew 18:21-22**, it is written, *"Then Peter came to him and asked, "Lord, how often should I forgive someone who sins against me? "Seven times?" "No!" Jesus replied, "seventy times seven!"*

4. Forgiveness is an ongoing process and even the smallest hurts you've experienced in the past may be causing you pain now. You may have to continually go back and forgive all over again until you've put the pain well behind you.

5. Accept the faults of others as well as your own and be ready to forgive. Jesus said, *"But when you are praying, first forgive anyone you are holding a grudge against, so that your Father in heaven will forgive your sins, too."* Mark 11:25- 26

As humans, forgiving someone is a difficult assignment indeed. It's not all about forgiving others but also about our own spiritual growth process. We cannot separate love and forgiveness and believe we will be better off. We have a choice, and as sinners, choosing God's ultimate love should be our sole purpose in life so forgiving is not an option we can easily avoid.

Here are a two bible verses that define forgiveness. As you read them, understand that it is up to us to make the first move because as we first forgive then we will be forgiven of our sins.

Matthew 6:14-15 – *"For if you forgive men when they sin against you, your heavenly Father will also forgive you. But if you do not forgive men their sins, your Father will not forgive your sins."*

Ephesians 4:31-32, *"Get rid of all bitterness, rage and anger, brawling and slander, along with every form of malice. Be kind and compassionate to one another, forgiving each other, just as in Christ God forgave you."*

The true act of forgiving others... being able to let go with both your heart and mind, creates a much healthier body and a mind free of anger and hate. Research has determined that when you are able to forgive, your blood pressure instantly goes down and those destructive feelings that cause pain are greatly minimized.

None of us can live with the stress of holding a grudge for a lifetime. Have you ever met those people who still hold a grudge? Have you seen how destructive they act, especially to others?

These types of people are so full of anger and rage that it seems they hold a grudge against the world They are angry all the time and blame all their problems on the one they hold the grudge against.

The numerous health benefits of forgiving others can be felt in the days and weeks following episodes of forgiveness.

1. Fewer bouts of muscle aches and headaches
2. Better sleep patterns
3. A higher resistance to disease
4. Better self-esteem
5. Closer personal relationships with family and friends.
6. Better concentration
7. Better eating habits (less likely to put on weight)
8. Less chance of confrontational behavior
9. Much less stress, anger, and bouts of depression

There is no excuse for not forgiving as it is in you to lay the groundwork for forgiveness. Whether for a lasting peace, a healthier state of mind, and grace from God, forgiveness is at the root of all love.

HOW DO I LET GO OF THE PAIN?

*"One word frees us of all the weight
and pain in life. That word is love."*
—Sophocles

Letting go of your emotional pain certainly has its benefits. Every act of forgiveness has value because forgiveness is not about placing blame on others or yourself. It's all about letting go of the chains that bind you and moving on with your life.

Forgiveness means you're able to recognize that the past is gone and can never come back and you can't let it take over your life. Forgiveness is a clean slate to start a new chapter in your life.

Another way we are able to let go is to be aware of our thoughts and recognize we need to watch what we think and the types of emotions we are feeling while not letting them take over our lives.

I can vividly remember when I was younger how my thoughts would take over my body and get me angry all over again. I'd become tense and irrational and it got me into a lot of trouble. I wouldn't pay attention to what I was doing at work and I'd make stupid and clumsy mistakes. I'd say all the wrong things to people I came in contact with because of the pain I was feeling. I was a real mess! It was killing me and I didn't know where to turn.

Then it happened. I saw myself for what I was becoming and I didn't like it at all. I decided right there and then I wanted a divorce from those negative thoughts and feelings which were paralyzing me. I started forgiving all those that hurt me. I finally asked for forgiveness from those that I hurt. It was truly liberating.

The trick is to pay close attention to what you are thinking about and when those feelings start to invade your thoughts create a mantra that you can use to zap those thoughts on the spot.

It could be as easy as a word or two such as, **"Be Gone"** or **"You Will Not Control Me."** These are target words that you can use to force your mind to avoid those negative thoughts. Anything to keep your thought patterns on the positive. That way, you will be in control not your negative thoughts.

This is what I did. I created those mantras to alert myself every time I felt the sting of the negative thoughts.

Your thoughts play a big role in your every day demeanor and if you're feeling down it will be conveyed to others. If you always smile, even when you're not feeling well, there is a much better chance you will not say the wrong things at the wrong time.

For many people, they let their thoughts and emotions guide their lives and they get into trouble for it. Forgiveness takes away the negativity and allows you to be more in control of what you do and say.

Did you know that the greatest power we have inside of us is the power to control our thoughts and emotions? It is this power that will help you elevate to a higher level and manifest in your conscious decisions. The decision to forgive is one of the deepest powers and when done correctly can free you of the burden of anger, resentment, and guilt.

But who has given you that power to control your emotions? Forgiveness is control but the ultimate control should be turned over to God so that he can take the pain and anger you feel and replace it with a love so rich and so strong that nothing can overcome it.

Here Are 4 Ways You Can Control Your Emotions And Free Yourself Of Pain.

1. Acknowledge that you have these types of emotions. Don't fight them as if they are the enemy. Instead, try to stand back and see your emotions for what they are... a basic part of what makes you, you. This means validate the fact that you have both good and bad emotions and know that they are just emotions.

2. Experience your emotions but don't reject them for this increases pain and causes you to give in to tits power. If you are driven by every emotion you have you cannot make logical choices. When negative emotions come, feel but do not act. Let them be part of you but not all of you.

3. Don't act on your emotions every time they bubble up to the surface. Take a deep breath and sit with them until they pass. When you hang onto your emotions they will get the better of you. If you open yourself up to them you become vulnerable. This vulnerability leads to anger, and anger leads to resentment, and this in turn, leads to hate.

4. Focus on solutions to how you are feeling, not what you are feeling. Decide on a course of action and fulfill it. Recognize that you are not your emotions and that you have the power to overcome your emotional state by recognizing the negative emotions when they appear.

The true act of forgiveness is not a war that you are fighting with everyone else but one that plays on your fear of being hurt all over again. You don't have to shy away from it. Instead, make a commitment to focusing on ending your negative thoughts when they appear while acknowledging they are part of you.

This is something you should be practicing all the time. The more you do it the more you will see the power that emotions have over you will diminish. Pain is something we all suffer from but you have the power within you to make forgiveness a part of becoming emotionally pain-free.

OVERCOMING RESENTMENT

*"Strength of character means the ability to overcome resentment
against others, to hide hurt feelings, and to forgive quickly."*
—Lawrence G. Lovasik

T he root of all resentment lies within us, not those who cause us to be filled with anger and hate. Ego is the biggest instigator of resentment and when we can reel in our ego, we can cure resentment. The problem is, most people would rather give in and let those feelings rule their heart.

When we defend our ego we lose sight of who we are and it takes us out of our state of grace. Once out of this state we are prone to sin and the effects it has on us. The key is to actively understand what those emotions are and then forgiving both the person we feel the resentment for and then ourselves.

Dr. Drew Pinsky, host of the popular radio call-in show called **"Loveline"** says this about resentment: ***"Resentments are like swallowing poison and expecting the other people to die."***

This poison is what I was experiencing every day of my life and I couldn't find a way to silence the anger. Anger, fear and resentment are all interconnected and trap us in an obsession-filled cycle where we hold on to the resentments of the past, angry with our present life, and afraid of what tomorrow may bring.

What Is The Antidote To This Poison?

When you are afraid, have faith in the Lord. When you are angry with someone or something, show them love and when you still feel resentment, offer up your acceptance of the situation to God and know that it's over right there. You can't do anything else to bring it back so leave it up to God.

Overcoming the resentments you have is an ongoing process. There is no magic pill that will heal you of the wounds but there are things you can do to start dealing with them in a way that helps you get on with your life.

Remember, it may get worse before it gets better. I didn't say it would be easy because it requires patience, a willingness to be healed, an open mind to work on your resentments, and a strong faith in God.

Finally, you need to be honest with yourself. One thing that harboring resentments does to us is it warps our sense of being honest with what happened in the past. If you are honest with yourself, healing comes much quicker and is less painful.

For me, that healing came much quicker when I put my resentment to paper. I took a four step approach to my resentments by laying it all out in front of me.

1. The first thing I did was to take a piece of paper and divide the top into four even sections. On the first section, I made a list of everyone and everything that has ever caused me resentment over the years. This was very painful but it needed to be done.

    It opened up some old wounds but I was able to flush out all the hurt and pain that had built up inside. I went back as far as I could remember and listed them in chronological order, noting that nothing was too insignificant because we all know it's the little things that irritate us the most.

2. In section two, I wrote down what these people did to me so I had a clear and concise record of the events. Why is this important? It helped bring those resentments out into the open. Those negative thoughts in

my head are one thing but seeing it with my own eyes forced me to deal directly with the pain.

3. The third section paired the negative emotions I had with each person and event. This made me well aware of how the resentment was messing with my mind and my ability to deal with life in general.

4. The final section was the toughest. I had to be totally honest with myself and admit my role in contributing to the problem. What had I done to make this become such a debilitating emotional problem and what could I have done to avoid it? Seeing it in front of me and admitting my guilt made me realize my own selfishness in the process and gave me a chance to start the healing process by having a clearer picture of who and what I resented.

By breaking down the entire process like this, you start the transition into identifying when and where resentment renders its ugly head. When you feel it happening and what it does to you, there is a much better chance you can control the way your emotions react to certain situations.

The main reason why you do this exercise is to help you let go of the fears, the anger, and the hate that has built up inside of you over the years. You'll be better equipped to handle the triggers that bring on the resentments and you can act more like a rational person when dealing with the flood of emotions that come your way.

As an added benefit to this exercise, start a journal. Everytime you have these resentments, write them down in the four-step procedure. This way, you deal with them as they happen and you avoid the buildup of emotional pain and anger that ultimately comes with resentment.

Throughout my life I clung to my resentments like a baby clings to its mother. No matter how hard I tried, those resentments wouldn't cease.

By lifting up my resentments to God, it gave me the strength to deal with all the garbage I had allowed to crowd my mind and heart. Once empty, it became much easier to forgive and move on.

THE REVENGE FACTOR

"There is no revenge so complete as forgiveness."
—Josh Billings

R evenge will never get you anywhere and it's an action that will only create more pain in your life. Remember, you want to create love, not invite hate.

Revenge also sabotages any effort to create peace in your own heart and it brings nothing of value to the table. The key here is to act in everyone's best interest, not just your own. Make your acts be acts of love and it will help you to move forward and create your own source of happiness.

Did you know that we have over 60,000 thoughts per day and that 80% of those thoughts are negative? But what's worse is the fact that over 90% of those negative thoughts are thoughts we have thought about before!

With revenge, our thoughts are stuck squarely in the past. All we want is to get back at the other person without thinking of the consequences. When you change your though patterns you can overcome those negative thoughts and see that revenge is stupid and nothing good can come from it.

Our hopes and dreams are all based on positive thoughts yet we let revenge stick to us like glue. Have you ever tried to talk to someone who has a grudge on someone? They are steadfast in their anger, have tunnel vision with their perception, and cannot overcome their hate.

According to psychologists, the act of revenge is like any other psychological need we have. It can't be numbed like you would with a shot or act like it doesn't exist. The only way to get over revenge is to find a healthy way to satisfy that same need.

Studies have shown that those who exact their revenge don't feel any better for it. In fact, many times they feel even worse for exacting revenge.

The best revenge you can ultimately hope for is fulfilling your life's destiny and become the person *YOU* want to be! No one can take that away from you and no one can deprive you of the love you have.

One of the greatest examples of how forgiveness and not revenge can show God's undying love for us came from **Pope John Paul II** after he was shot by **Mehmet Ali Agca**, a Turkish assassin who was sent to kill the Pope.

Ali Agca shot the Pope six times and nearly killed him but after he was arrested by Italian authorities, Ali Agca was visited by the Pope in jail and was completely forgiven. Mehmet Ali Agca later converted to Christianity and 31 years to the day, left a bouquet of flowers on the Pope's tomb as an act of love.

Ali Agca was taken aback by the Pope's pure and unselfish love and couldn't understand why the Pope had forgiven him. It was a great act of mercy and forgiveness which showed what the power of love can do. The Pope didn't exact revenge, but showed unconditional love which was so foreign to Ali Agca. Only after being forgiven did he understand the true power of love.

Lewis Smedes, author of **"The Art of Forgiving"** once remarked, *"Forgiveness happens inside the person doing the forgiving. It heals our pain and resentment before it does anything for the person we forgive; they might never know about it."*

You have to take it upon yourself to make forgiveness a part of your everyday habit. Why let things fester and boil over when you can open up your heart and make it go away? You have the power... so use it.

In the **Lord's Prayer** it is written, *"Forgive us our trespasses as we forgive those who trespass against us."* Those powerful words show us how we are supposed to act and what happens when we fail to forgive. What we are praying for is mercy. Mercy for our own cause as well as mercy for others... for without out it, neither of us can experience real forgiveness.

It is in those words that we take forgiveness to the next level. Forgive, forget and move on...

DISCOVER THE JOYS OF
APPRECIATION AND GRATITUDE

"The one thing we can never get enough of is love.
And the one thing we never give enough is love."
—Henry Miller

W hy is appreciation so important to understanding love? Where does appreciation come from and why should we be so appreciative in the first place?

I have thought a lot about this over the years and have seen what real appreciation is. From people I don't even know to those I come in contact with everyday, being appreciative is a very important part of sharing love.

Feeling like we are genuinely appreciated lifts us up and makes us feel safe in our personhood. Without appreciation, we lose our unique value in this world, it drains our positive energy, and we cannot reach our true potential as a person.

Jack Canfield, the bestselling author of **"Chicken Soup For The Soul"** tells us that, *"A state of appreciation is one of highest vibrational emotional states possible."*

Appreciation is an act that comes from deep within our heart. When we create the effort to appreciate life and those in it, we make our relationships with others much healthier

But, where does appreciation actually come from?

I believe the most important part of being appreciated and showing appreciation comes from humility. Humility is a very formidable word and yet it's a concept that most people do not fully comprehend.

Why is that?

Being humble comes from an inner strength but most people I have spoken with seem to think you need to be meek and non-aggressive to be humble. They are so wrong!

Being humble means giving up on being selfish and concentrating on others, whether it is for their well-being, listening instead of talking, or putting others first.

Many of us have seen these types of people and wish we could be more like them. They seem to have an aura about them that is calm and inviting. They show love in everything they do and it comes across so naturally.

Humility is a conscious decision to put others first and we show our appreciation of others in how we treat them. It is also about our awareness of life itself. Those that are more observant tend to see more value in others and can see the bigger picture when dealing with the importance of everyone they come into contact with.

Humility is a lifestyle, not just living moment by moment. Those that practice it are more optimistic about life and continually see opportunities to serve others.

Humility has always been a dilemma to me. As much as I knew what it meant to be humble, doing so was another thing altogether. I never felt like I could give enough of myself so I did not think I had the strength to be humble until I read this quote which changed my thinking 180 degrees from author and professor, **David Bobb**, who said, **"Humility is a great force of hidden strength."**

Finding this hidden strength is the key to being humble. It took me years to find that hidden strength. Throughout the ages, those that master this strength become very successful in their lives.

Take the great **Dale Carnegie** for instance. In his book, "**How To Win Friends And Influence People**", he mentions that *"Honest and sincere appreciation is the secret to getting along with people."* In fact, this quote by **William James** sums it up perfectly, *"The deepest craving in human nature is the craving to be appreciated."*

Let's delve more into how humility and appreciation are so closely related and how you can use them to become the person you've always wanted to be.

WHY IS HUMILITY SO IMPORTANT TO LOVE?

"There is no respect for others without humility in one's self."
—Henri Frederic Amiel

What difference can humility make in our lives?

There is no greater enemy to humility than pride and pride leads to arrogance. Once we walk in arrogance we lose our grace with God. It is the mortal enemy of our souls.

On the other hand, humility allows the Lord to enter into our hearts and work through us. **John MacArthur**, from **"The Grace To You"** blog, speaks of how humility is seen in the new millennium. *"We live in a very proud and egotistical generation. It is now considered acceptable and even normal for people to promote themselves, to praise themselves, and to put themselves first. Pride is considered a virtue by many. Humility, on the other hand, is considered a weakness. Everyone, it seems, is screaming for his or her own rights and seeking to be recognized as someone important."*

83

If we continue being prideful, love won't grow. It's as easy as that! When we seek our own glory and greatness we walk away from truth. Without that truth, showing real love to others is impossible.

During my lowest period, I thought I could handle my anger and hate but my pride wouldn't allow me to go for help. Once I was able to focus on my humility I found solace in forgiveness.

The unselfishness that comes with humility is something that needs to be experienced. Humility is not a natural state of affairs with humans. In fact, it has to be learned and many of us have not yet learned from those painful lessons of the past.

All human relationships depend on humility. With humility, a humble person makes room for other people in their lives. **Sirach**, one of my favorite Biblical authors, puts it all in perspective, *"Conduct your affairs with humility and you will be loved more than a giver of gifts." - Sirach 3:17*

Humility begins with trust. A trust that submits to the imitation of our Lord and gives you the power to treat others in such a way that uplifts and puts them first. This type of love is hard to come by but it really is a simple concept. It is recognizing the ultimate truth: God is love and to humble ourselves before Him knowing full well we are all sinners. Once you recognize that and put it into practice, you will see the fruits of your own love.

Here Are 5 Positive Effects Of Humility In Your Life

1. **It soothes your soul** - Humility brings on a quiet perspective about who we are and how we relate to others. This perspective also allows us to be more attuned to the needs of others.

2. **It gives you self control** - Studies have found that the more humble a person is, the better they are at exhibiting self control in any given situation. Humility allows us to know our limits and act upon them.

3. **Better work and school performance** - Studies once again show that those who practice humility do better in school and are better suited to perform their duties at work.

4. **Humble people are also less prejudice towards others** - Humility spawns tolerance which leads to a less prejudice view of people and their surroundings. One of the main characteristics of being humble is being less defensive about one's own beliefs and a more willingness to respect others views and property.

5. **Humble people are more generous** - Again, studies show the more humble we are, the more we give of ourselves. From helping others to charitable donations, humble people give because they want to, not because they are forced to.

6. **Humility breeds togetherness** - Humble people are better at building and maintaining relationships because of their willingness to accept others for who they are. The act of humility also helps repair torn relationships and builds stronger bonds between people no matter where they come from.

7. **7: Humility comes from fear of the Lord** - *Proverbs 22:4* states *"Humility is the fear of the Lord; its wages are riches and honor and life."* To honor God we give of ourselves through humility. The Lord in turn rewards our humility with all of his riches, horror, and life. What more can you ask for?

The better and stronger bonds of friendship and care you build, the more love you release into the world. These small pockets of love are like balloons as they fly off into the distance bringing people closer together.

According to **Confucius**, *"Humility is the solid foundation of all virtues."* It is in the act of being virtuous that we see the love of others. These virtues help focus your energies where they do the most good.

When we are truly humble we draw people to us. Humility breeds kindness which builds and fosters peace among people. Without a solid foundation, any love you try to give out to the world has nothing of substance behind it.

Andrew Murray, author of **"Humility: The Beauty Of Holiness"** states this about humility: *"Humility is not so much a grace or virtue along with others; it is the root of all, because it alone takes the right attitude before God, and allows Him as God to do all.... It is simply the sense of entire nothingness, which comes when we see how truly God is all, and in which we make way for God to be all."*

As you can see, God is the magic formula for making humility work in your life. Engage others in love and the fruits of the **Holy Spirit** will bless you each and every day.

THE LOVING ACT
OF APPRECIATION

*"Appreciation is a wonderful thing: It makes
what is excellent in others belong to us as well."*
—Voltaire

S ometimes, we get so caught up in looking for appreciation that we forget
that being appreciated is a step in caring about others. Being appreciated
isn't a bad thing. Deep down, most of us crave appreciation for the things
we do and get upset when we aren't appreciated for all that we have done.

Ever felt that way in life? Of course you have. It is a natural part of life but
when someone goes all out and shows their full appreciation for us we sometimes
don't know how to receive that appreciation in a positive light.

What makes accepting appreciation so hard?

Mike Robbins, the well-respected motivational speaker who talks a lot
about appreciation, both giving and receiving, blogged about what happened
on his 40th birthday.

His wife went all out for his birthday celebration and had family and friends record a special video of how much they appreciated him and how much they cared about him. He then shared how hard it was to show his own appreciation because of his humbleness but he realized it goes far beyond that.

He describes how we as humans, have to two responses to being appreciated. The first is, we thank the person or persons and return the compliment and second, we dismiss the compliment because we don't think we measure up and even feel a little guilty at all the acclaim.

He goes on to say how he felt very insecure about his own form of reciprocation. Did he treat others that way for their birthday? Did he show love the way they showed him love? Was it warranted? Was he worthy of all the appreciation he received?

He asks this very probing question. *"How comfortable are we in receiving gratitude and accepting appreciation in our lives?" Appreciation can be very empowering for us. It can also heal the pain we have deep inside and finally, it is not only beneficial to us but it is an incredible experience for the other person."*

You see, it goes both ways and that opens up various avenues of love that weren't there before. He went on to say that this type of appreciation and gratitude has been shown to the raise the serotonin levels of both parties involved. It makes everyone happier and lowers stress levels.

The problem I see is we don't know how to accept all that love and appreciation in a way that helps us grow to be happier and healthier human beings. And taking that a step further, the more genuine (key word here) love we can show the world, the more it will be reciprocated our way and the happier we all will be.

The act of appreciation stimulates the flow of love that is around us. As long as we apply it to our daily lives we will see positive results. It is important for us to do it every day and not just *want* to make the commitment.

Appreciation comes in many forms. Making a difference in other's lives by being a good friend may be the most important gesture you can make in appreciating what the world has given you. It's passing on the love you have to someone who really needs it.

When you are able to express your appreciation for things others have done for you, their lives are greatly enhanced and it enriches your own life in a way that fulfills everyone involved.

I have seen firsthand what happens when you show interest in others. They are drawn to you in such a way as to want to build stronger relationships. That idea is the cornerstone of building and keeping long-lasting friendships.

Everyone wants to feel appreciated and when you offer that kind of care to another person it releases more love into the world. Position yourself to appreciate things more.

This quote from **Charlie "Tremendous" Jones** goes right to the heart of what true appreciation is. *"If you are not grateful for what you have right now, what makes you think you'll be any more grateful if you have more?"*

Those are strong words indeed. How grateful are you for the things you already have? Will having more make you happier? Appreciation comes too late when you've lost everything. That is why you need to understand that real wealth is not made of possessions but what you have been given by God.

Each gift of appreciation is like a beat of your heart. It gives and gives and keeps you going. Appreciation is the gift that everyone is grateful for.

Appreciation can be shown in the smallest of gestures and former President, **John F. Kennedy** put it best when he said, *"As we express our gratitude, we must never forget that the highest appreciation is not to utter words, but to live by them."*

How you live by them is what makes showing love that much easier.

HOW TO BE MORE APPRECIATIVE

"The roots of all goodness lie in the soil of appreciation for goodness."
—Dalai Lama

Being more appreciative of what we have goes much further than just physical and tangible items. It goes to the very heart of who we are and what we believe in.

When you appreciate what Jesus did upon the cross you can appreciate all the love he has for us… Both the sacrifices and commitments he made on our behalf for our own good. The same goes for what we have and what we do with it.

What are you thankful for and what are you most appreciative of?

Some might say their health, check. Some might say their families, check. Others may be thankful they have a job while those less fortunate will be thankful for food on the table.

In the Philippines, I have witnessed how the poor live and it breaks my heart. I've been so moved at how thankful they are for what they have and will even share with you the little they do have.

Look, you never know when things may change for the worse in your life and you can't really plan for bad things to happen so it's crucial to be appreciative of what you have at this point in time.

Many people take for granted the good things in their lives and don't think about appreciation until it's way too late. When you start looking for things to be grateful for, you begin to appreciate all the simple pleasures you previously took for granted.

Taking this a bit further is a quote by **Meister Eckhart,** *"If the only prayer you said in your whole life was, 'thank you,' that would suffice."*

This is a very important thing to remember. Since my accident I have a much greater appreciation for life. And I do believe that much more since two more tragedies have happened since my own accident.

My youngest daughter plays on a travelling soccer team and one of her teammates lost her father to a brain aneurysm. One day he was alive and the next he was gone. He was a great person who coached both the girls' soccer and basketball teams and was much loved among parents and kids alike.

The second tragedy happened to one of my oldest daughter's best friends from high school. She was only seventeen and had just gotten her driver's license. Going to work after school, she was killed in a horrific car accident. She was one of the nicest and most caring young ladies I have ever met. We cried for a very long time after that but as I said, show appreciation to those you care about for they may not be there one day.

Here Are 5 Ways You Can Incorporate Appreciation Into Your Daily Life

1. **Prayer** - When you pray from the heart, thank God for what you have. Your humility is what allows you to thank God for all the bounty he has given you.
2. **Write down all those things you are truly thankful for** - The act of writing down what you are thankful for is a physical reminder that forces you to see the good in your own life. Keep adding to this list when something good comes to you.
3. **Make a concerted and genuine effort to show your appreciation** – That effort is important in showing others on a regular basis, even if it is just a quick thank you for something someone has done for you.

4. **Train yourself to look for the good in everyone and everything** - This allows us to see others more fully... such as the good qualities that we may have overlooked before.

5. **Always try to end your day on a positive note** - It's much healthier for you and you will relieve much of the day's stress just by putting yourself in a positive mindset.

So where does appreciation lead to?

FINDING GRATITUDE
IN EVERYDAY LIFE

*"Gratitude makes sense of our past, brings peace
for today, and creates a vision for tomorrow."*
—Melody Beattie

Gratitude is the next logical step. What you value you should give back in return, that way it continuously multiplies. You should live your life with total gratitude for what you have been given and not worry about what you don't have. The intention is to give with a generous heart and receive with a grateful heart.

Some days, the stresses in our life make it almost impossible to live with a grateful heart. I understand life is hard but making it harder only inhibits our interactions with others.

Wouldn't it be wonderful if you could set in motion the wheels of gratitude by doing something nice for someone else and inspiring them to pass it on?

Many times I have read where motorists have paid the toll for the person behind them and each successive car returns the favor until everyone is concentrating on giving and not worrying about their own situation.

The opportunities to give back to the world are limitless and using your thoughtfulness can bring out the love that others may have overlooked in you.

When I first brought my wife here to America from the Philippines, I wanted to give her the best life I could but it just wasn't possible on my salary. It also didn't help that we lived in an old broken-down apartment building on the first floor which was partially set underground. When we looked outside we could barely see the front yard. We felt like we had one foot in the grave already.

By the fifth month of our lease, the bathroom started peeling paint and the shower was leaking water every time we used it. This wasn't the kind of life I had envisioned giving her but we were grateful for what we had. Through hard work, patience and a whole lot of prayers, we eventually bought the house of our dreams and when we look back on those early days, we smile because we know how blessed we really are.

This is exactly what I'm trying to show you. Appreciate what you have for you may not have it in the future. For example, we have many friends from the Philippines who lost loved ones in Typhoon Haiyan back in 2013. It was one of the deadliest typhoons to ever hit that country.

Thousands of people died and tens of thousands either lost everything they had or were displaced from their homes. We were very lucky as her relatives were not along the path but others were not quite as fortunate.

In everything we do, love should be the main reason we do it. It is the most powerful force the universe has ever known. It creates abundance and it can heal what ails you but you must first invite it into your life.

German theologian and Lutheran pastor **Dietrich Bonhoeffer** states, *"Gratitude changes the pangs of memory into a tranquil joy."* We sometimes look at gratitude when things are going well but have you ever looked at it when your live has given you obstacles to overcome?

It is in the bad times that we rely on help from the Lord above to change our position in life but sometimes we need to go through the bad times to appreciate the good times.

My life completely changed after my car accident. The physical pain I was feeling couldn't compare to the emotional pain that had engulfed my life over the years. It was only when I realized how blessed I was that I was still alive and had my family with me that I could appreciate what I had been given.

When I accepted my pain and then decided to change my heart that was when I found out how important gratitude really was. Oh, I had practiced gratitude before and was thankful for everything I had but it wasn't till it was almost taken away that gratitude became an important part of my life.

That accident was my coming out party and I now practice positive acts of gratitude and my prayers are full of appreciation and gratitude for what God has given me. Like they say, you don't know what you have until it's taken away. In my case, I finally understand how I'm supposed to live.

Practice the joys of forgiveness, appreciation, and gratitude and you will be that much closer to love.

LIVING A LIFE OF THANKSGIVING

*"Gratitude is the inward feeling of kindness received.
Thankfulness is the natural impulse to express that
feeling. Thanksgiving is the following of that impulse."*
—Henry Van Dyke

Each day gives us a chance to be thankful for everything we have. If we decide that everything we do comes from our own hard work then we could never achieve anything of significance. I've seen firsthand that it's divine providence looking over our shoulders and watching out for us than my own hard work.

After my accident, I am forever living in thanksgiving because I was given a second chance at life. Things like this do not happen haphazardly. God has a plan for each one of us and when we deviate from that plan we get ourselves in trouble.

What are you thankful for?

Do you make it known in prayer and supplication for the many blessings you have received? I know I'm not the only one who has been given a second chance at life but I know what I am thankful for. Besides the **Lord Jesus Christ**, it's my family, my friends, my job, and my health. I make sure I let God know how thankful I am for everything I have.

Thanksgiving is not just another form of appreciation as it goes much deeper than that. Thanksgiving goes right to the heart of everything we do. It is cuts through all the haze in our lives and puts the emphasis directly where it should be… on God.

If you are not thankful for what you have in your life then may I ask why not? Is it too much trouble to be thankful for having a roof over your head, food on the table, and a job to take care of your family?

We take things for granted far too much and when something bad happens to us we push blame on someone else. It's as if we blame someone else for us losing control over our lives. The funny thing is we never really have full control over anything. If we did, we'd screw things up much more than we already do!

If you're not thankful for what you have now, how do you bring thanksgiving into your life?

First of all, thanksgiving is grounded in unselfishness. Selfish people don't know how to be thankful for what they have. Secondly, thanksgiving comes from the heart. It's a way of living and being. It does not come from how much we get or our lot in life. It is all about living a life based on being thankful for what we do have and for how we've been treated.

When we begin to pray, our prayers should be prayers of thanksgiving first and foremost. They should be filled with praise and thanks for God's goodness. We pray not for what we want but for what we've been given. That's the difference here. Those who are unhappy have no feelings of thanksgiving and that further adds to their unhappiness.

Thanksgiving also creates calmness in our lives. It brings us a genuine amount of love into your life. Thanksgiving is a way to heal what ails your heart.

Thanksgiving is more than just a holiday for those that show gratitude, because it's a way of life. **Bo Baker**, a highly successful Executive Coach, Leadership Consultant, and keynote speaker once said, *"Thanksgiving is grace dressed in unselfishness, gratitude spelled out in personal concern and character showing its colors like the lovely leaves of fall."*

The whole goal of being thankful is the natural response to grace and the goodness of a wonderful God who cares enough to provide all that we need.

When our lives are broken, we have trouble feeling thankful but those who put thanksgiving first in their lives are promised great blessings in the bible as mentioned in **Ezekiel 34:26**, *"God blesses you so you can be a blessing to others! "I will cause my people and their homes around my holy hill to BE a blessing. And I will send showers, showers of blessings, which will come just when they are needed."*

There will be problems in our lives but it is for our own good that these things happen to us. These trials have their purpose and when we go through these trials, it strengthens our faith and love for God. He helps bring us to a new state of love.

Thanksgiving is a way of celebrating our happiness. If you can see the good in everything instead of complaining, see problems as opportunities to grow in love then the opportunities for healing are well within your grasp.

Can you imagine the kind of world it would be where everyone was thankful for everything they had? The evolution of gratitude would bring about so much happiness in mankind which could bring about true inner peace for the whole world.

Inner peace depends on us being thankful. There is so much for us to experience that when our lives are in upheaval, we only have once place to look to make us whole again.

When my life was in total disorder, I thought there was nothing I could do to find peace but when my accident came, I realized I had to give control of my life back over to Jesus. Since then, so many great things have happened to me that I know the key to healing lies in God's unconditional love.

Thanksgiving really means knowing that whatever you do, God will give you what you need to live a blessed life. In **James 1:17**, *"Every good thing given and every perfect gift is from above, coming down from the Father of lights, with whom there is no variation or shifting shadow."*

Live like thanksgiving has already been given and love like you have already been blessed and your blessings will never end.

STEP 2

PUTTING LOVE
INTO ACTION

HOW TO SAY NO TO SELFISHNESS
AND YES TO SELFLESSNESS

"The love we give away is the only love we keep."
—Elbert Hubbard

W hen there is no love in your life you feel empty, lonely and are filled with pain and resentment. Your life is filled with chaos but this all changes when love is ever present.

For as long as I can remember, I felt like I had no love in my life. I'm not talking about having a girlfriend or dating but the true feeling that other people actually cared about me, were willing to stick up for me, and were there for me when I needed them.

It was no fun being alone but it's even worse when you feel like you can't approach anyone without feeling like you've already been rejected.

The truest form of love is unselfish love. The kind of love that is wholly unconditional. It is a love that gives first, and last, and always in between.

101

When we are so absorbed in our own lives, it kills our ability to be empathetic to the plights of others and we lack compassion. Our world becomes all that is important to us and we are preoccupied with our own problems.

For years, I was preoccupied with my own problems and I realized how far I had pushed everyone else away. It was scary looking back on it because I saw how much my life was devoid of joy but more importantly, how much I was turning everyone else off.

The key here is to focus on others so that we lift both ourselves and others up together. The problems we encounter won't seem as important and we increase our full capacity for selfless action.

Joshua Becker, best-selling author of the book, **"The More Of Less"** states *"Selflessness is an important key to marriage, friendships, and relationships. It is also an essential key to happiness and fulfillment. But unfortunately, often overlooked."*

We overlook it because selflessness doesn't further our own selfish agenda. Instead, Joshua goes on to say, *"May we refuse to overlook the importance of selflessness. Instead, may we choose to pursue selflessness as the very means to achieve happiness - not just for our own sake, but for the sake of those we choose to love."*

God's happiness always overtakes our own version of what we think happiness is. By digging deeper into what selflessness entails we can bring God's happiness into our own life.

In **Mathew 20:16**, the Bible tells us, *"In the same way, the last will be first, and the first will be last, because many are called, but few are chosen."*

Be one of the chosen and love that way. Live to serve for it is in the service that we find and distribute this wonderful love.

So the next obvious question is how do I put others first without forgetting myself?

HOW TO SERVE OTHERS FIRST

*"To live a pure unselfish life, one must count
nothing as one's own in the midst of abundance."*
—Buddha

Putting others first doesn't mean just being a nice person. It's a sincere attitude that you care enough to honor others before yourself. It is a way of acting that promotes friendship and love. It doesn't mean forgetting ourselves and our own needs but seeing an opportunity for service.

Service is the key word here for without serving others our whole world becomes limited to own experiences. We need to find a way to empower others with love.

Service gives us a real sense of pride and purpose by doing everything we can to enhance our world. To serve others is to serve God.

From **Ephesians 2:10,** we learn that *"It is God himself who has made us what we are and given us new lives from Christ Jesus; and long ages ago he planned that we should spend these lives in helping others."*

Here are a few examples that can help you do this as well as understanding the concept of selflessness.

1. **Practice the art of putting yourself last** – Being selfish means always putting yourself first but that doesn't help anyone. Instead, live a life filed with joy where you make others feel special. When you think of others first, you will be blessed by others. They will see how unselfish you are and will be there for you when you are in need.

    Zig Zigler, One of the greatest marketers and motivational speakers to ever live, made these two statements below and they are how I live my life today.

    "You will get all you want in life, if you help enough other people get what they want."

    "The way you see people is the way you treat them."

    These two statements sum up what we all should be doing while we are here on this earth, yet you and I both know, very few people live that way. In fact, I'm surprised when I encounter someone who embodies these principles because I am not used to seeing people act in this manner.

    We're all guilty of how we mistreat others. It could be saying the wrong thing at the wrong time, not supporting someone when they really need it, or even not acknowledging something they've done or accomplished.

    No one wants to be mistreated but when we see people in a particular way (especially if we've been hurt in the past) we tend to judge based on how we were treated and subconsciously end up treating them the same exact way. It's a vicious cycle that continues unless we can take a step back and recognize the symptoms.

    If you can change the way you view people then you change the way you treat them. This, in turn, will change how you deal with people and how they ultimately deal with you.

    This one change can mean a world of difference in being able to love others. When you feel loved you are able to give love much easier.

    I find it very refreshing to meet these types of individuals because they are an inspiration to me. They make it easier to accept my own problems when they show their selflessness.

2. **Practice the art of walking in someone's shoes** - Each of us has our own tribulations but when we try to understand what others are feeling and going through in any given situation, we discover that our own problems don't seem to be all that important.

    The more you practice understanding people's situations the more you will be able to put aside your own brand of selfishness and provide love to others.

    Let me give you an example of how this works.

    Let's say, you go out for dinner and you want it to be a beautiful experience with your spouse or significant other and everything is going great. The restaurant is very crowded and your waitress brings you the wrong item from the menu. How do you react?

    Do you get mad at her for giving you the wrong order or do you think about her plight? For all you know, she could be working more than one job trying to provide for her family. Maybe something very sad has just happened in her life (a death in the family, a bad break-up, or even an unexpected bill that has made her situation even worse) which is causing her internal strife.

    It is times like these that we need to see beyond our own selfish concerns. By the way, this really happened to me and I wrote a little note on the back of the dinner bill with these words. **"Don't worry. You are loved!"** and I gave her an extra $20 on top of her regular tip. I wasn't rich at the time (and still aren't) but it was my way of showing empathy and love to someone whom I never met before. I wanted her to know that someone cared about her.

    I've been in that situation many times before in my life and I know how they feel. By empathizing with their situation and showing gratitude, I am able to pass along a small bit of love.

3. **Practice the art of being part of the universe, not the center of it** - No matter who you are, we have all been given certain talents, traits, and gifts by God and no one is more important than anyone else. The world doesn't revolve around us and we are no better than anyone else. We are all loved by God no matter who we are or what we have done.

    When we become part of the universe, we interact in a loving sort of way. By giving and taking love we help keep the balance flowing freely.

When we make ourselves the center of everything we push others to the side. Their hopes, their dreams, and their experiences become superfluous to us and we miss a vital part of what life is all about.

We all have a part to play in this life and if we hog the entire spotlight we miss the beauty going on around us. Now, some people may question your ulterior motives when you try to do something selfless but you need to learn to compromise and be tolerant.

There are many selfish people out there but that doesn't mean we need to compete with them. Let them have their temporary moment of glory while we support those who need it the most.

4. **Practice the art of listening -** Those that listen are more understanding to the plight of others. When you talk to others, try to make the conversation a more 50/50 exchange and you will pick up things about the other person you may never have known.

We all have problems and sometimes we need others input but selfish people monopolize conversations and go on and on about their own problems, struggles and setbacks and forget the other person may need a good listener to help them when life has got them down.

According to **Paul Sacco, Ph.D.**, an assistant professor at the University of Maryland School of Social Work, *"We all have a good listener within us. It all just depends on the ability and desire to be mindful of where you are and who you're talking to. A lot of us are focused on the mechanics of listening - eye contact, nodding your head - but for good listeners, there's naturalness to that behavior that we should all aspire to."*

When you listen, have an open mind. It allows you to be a better communicator. This quote by **Rachel Naomi Remen** sums it up perfectly… *"The most basic and powerful way to connect to another person is to listen. Just listen. Perhaps the most important thing we ever give each other is our attention."*

Whose attention are you giving?

Your own or someone else's? Get this right and people will instantly be attracted to you.

5. **Practice the art of taking an interest in other people's lives -** Find out what others are doing. Ask questions and take a keen interest in what they say and do. You can learn a lot from other people's experiences.

This is very true of older people. One thing I truly enjoy is hearing stories from the lives of my elders. Things such as where they came from, their struggles, what they enjoyed doing, and especially their life stories have always fascinated me.

One man, whom I met at the mall a few years back, came and sat down next to me. He was in his late eighties and looked tired so I introduced myself and started up a conversation.

He had taken out a block of wood and knife and started carving away. He told me all about his collection of wood carvings he made in his spare time. He said he loved to carve little wooden ships and learned the skill while he was in the Navy.

I could see the excitement in his eyes as we engaged in conversation. When I told him I enjoyed vacationing in places where I can be out near the water, he told me about his experiences in the Philippines while serving in the Navy.

Since my wife is from the Philippines, we connected on a much deeper level and had a great time talking about the different places we both had visited there. Had I not interacted with him, I would have not experienced the rich and vast knowledge he had to offer.

You see, we all have a lot to give and we can learn from other's experiences. My wife and I have made many lifelong friends from taking an interest in other people we've just met and making them feel important.

In fact, two of our children's godparents came from this very same way of treating others. Once we became friends, we showed our love in many different ways. That is reason why we take an interest in others… is to show unconditional love.

It takes a lot of patience to be selfless but it can do so much good for others. This is shown in the next art.

6. **Practice the art of taking on responsibilities** – Taking responsibility is very important to understanding the role love plays in our lives. One example of taking responsibility is having a pet. It is one of life's great pleasures but it also comes with great responsibility. Being responsible for their welfare, their safety, and their health is the greatest honor we can share for their unconditional love.

This is something we have always taught our children. When my youngest daughter was eleven years old, she and her best friend ran a pet sitting business for people who lived in our neighborhood. The girls both love dogs and learned a valuable lesson on being responsible.

We hold that same responsibility for our families. Never forget that the bond that holds our families together is based on responsibility. We are our brother's keeper and it is up to us to take care of our families no matter what!

Another type of responsibility is accepting what we've done in our life. Too many times we've blamed others for our past mistakes. Responsibility is the mark of maturity. Being mature is knowing we are not perfect and not trying to compare ourselves with others but accepting them for who they are. This is real love.

I know I've had a hard time stopping myself from blaming others. It was only when I decided to take responsibility for my own actions did I start accepting people for who they were.

When we are able to stop comparing ourselves to others, we take the next step and start doing for others. We should be looking for opportunities to show our love by helping those in need.

We all need to be responsible for ourselves and our family's welfare but how far should we take responsibility when it comes to others?

Taking on responsibility in the name of others is sharing the great idea of loving others. Once again, the bible is very specific about this.

In **Mark 12:30-31, Jesus** tells us, *"And you shall love the Lord your God with all your heart, and with all your soul, and with all your mind, and with all your strength." The second is this, "You shall love your neighbor as yourself. There is no other commandment greater than these."*

Our whole life is predicated on these two verses. Loving your neighbor should be just as important as loving yourself. If you get this right you will know what true love is.

THE SECRET TO ATTRACTING LOVE

*"Your mind is a magnet. You don't attract what
you need or what you want; you attract who you are!"*
—Carlos Santana

Y ou've probably heard of the Law Of Attraction and how it states that
your thoughts are manifested in your life as either positive or negative
experiences and you attract what you give out. Well, I want to take that
concept a step further.

When we focus our energies on something that is positive, more than likely
positive things will happen and the same goes with negative thoughts. The
problem with this type of behavior goes right back to the act of selfishness. This
is not to say that it is selfish to wish good things for ourselves but it is in the way
we go about it.

Let me give you a prime example:

Suppose you want something so bad you concentrate on it with
all your heart. You send positive thoughts out to the universe and you

believe deep inside you will get it and it finally happens. You get what you want. Great!

But what happens if you don't? Do you go right back to emanating negative energy and start feeling like you're not worthy or maybe even worse, you're angry at not getting what you want and you get mad at the word?

Why then are you focusing your energies on the negative aspect? Instead, refocus your energies on attracting good things in your life. Refocus your thoughts on things that are good and pure.

In this day and age, it seems to be all about being cool, promoting the bad-boy image and the *"I-me-mine"* attitude. We see it in all the magazines, television shows and even in our music.

Everyone loves reality shows, living the good life, and feeding their own voracious appetites. Commercials promote everything under the sun to seduce us and we fall victim to our own brand of selfish behavior.

Whatever happened to being a good person with proper morals?

Whatever happened to treating others with respect and care? We have gotten away from putting others first as it has become all about us in the new millennium.

Let's decide to be different. Let's attract love in everything we do. Let's not only change our thought patterns but how we view the world. Remember, you can't change others but you can change yourself. That comes first!

For many people, change is scary. Change is something most of us avoid because it doesn't cater to our egos. Ego and love don't mix and guess what… love loses out most of the time.

Persian poet and mystic **Jalal ad-Din Rumi** says this about love, *"Your task is not to seek for love, but merely to seek and find all the barriers within yourself that you have built against it."*

These barriers are all based on our egos and if we can keep them in check, love is well within our grasp. Attracting love is not about what we want but able what we are able to give.

Here Are 5 Things You Can Do To Attract Love Into Your Life

1. Be clear about the type of person you want to be. Do you want to be an affectionate, caring and considerate person? In order to attract those qualities in others we need to become that type of person who emanates love to others.

2. Let go of your old ways and remove those obstacles that are distracting you from allowing love to come into your hearts. Work on those things that keep you from bringing happiness into the world. Change is good when you focus your change on trusting in the Lord.

3. Embrace healing in your heart. Make a conscious commitment to start healing the deepest wounds in your heart. Tear down the walls of protection you've built up over the years and start welcoming goodness and love into your heart.

4. When your own pain is not an obstacle you are free to love others unconditionally. Always be willing to invite healing into your life and see how it attracts love.

5. Release your fears and limiting beliefs that keeps love from coming to you. Your insecurities play games with your mind and limit your opportunities to embrace love so work on eliminating those fears. Most of the time, those fears are unfounded and feel much scarier than they actually are.

6. Make room in your heart for love. Don't let love have to compete for your attention. Instead, let it occupy your heart and mind. As funny as it may sound, many people have trouble making room in their hearts for others because their egos just won't allow it. Welcome love with open arms and give it a chance. You never know what you may find.

For me, the law of attracting love was just a puzzle and I felt like I didn't have all the pieces. I searched but I didn't know what to look for. I hoped but I didn't open myself up to it and I prayed but I didn't believe.

What are you attracting, who are you attracting, and how are you attracting others in your life? If you can answer those three questions honestly, you can begin attracting a deeper kind of connection with others.

The Law Of Attraction states that you attract that which you most focus on. Start focusing on those things that are good, pure, and God based. If you let your ego take over you will never attract anything but negative energy and bad karma.

FOCUS ON OTHERS,
NOT POSSESSIONS

"We may give without loving, but we cannot love without giving."
—Bernard Meltzer

Be honest. What is the most important thing in your life?

Is it your money? Is it your house? How about a great job? Could it be your family? What about your friends?

You are what you think and therefore, you will act accordingly. If you concentrate on material issues you will never be happy.

Oh, I can see you cringe at the thought! So, what you are saying is, I should not make any money to take care of myself and my family?

That's a cop out and an excuse. Of course we should all do what we can to take care of ourselves and our family financially but it does come at a price.

How many people are in over their heads financially these days? How many people are so broke that all they do is work to pay off their big mortgage, huge car payments, and all the toys they have accumulated?

I remember when I was spending all my time writing my books because I wanted to make enough money to quit my day job but it came at a very steep price indeed. My youngest daughter would always come up to me and ask, *"Dad, why do you spend all your time writing? How come you never spend any time with us?"*

It broke my heart to hear her say that and I finally realized my family was my riches and I was throwing it all away by being selfish and greedy. I used to think that if I became a best-selling author I'd have it all but it didn't work out that way.

I once again realized that if I could use my gift to help others then I could spread my message of love and hope to those that really need it. By including my family in my writing I could spend quality time with them and teach them how to help others at the same time.

Just that small change of focus opened up brand new avenues to show my love. It opened up more time for my family and I was able to turn my love of writing into a new way to give back to others while still giving them the time and love they all deserved.

What can you do to show your love?

When you focus every part of life on yourself, you are never satisfied with what you have and will always be wanting more. If you want to stop putting the spotlight on yourself, you have to feel like you already have enough things in your life. Any extra gifts you receive should come as an added bonus.

And regarding those "extra gifts," I was always told to be a cheerful giver by sharing what I had. Which means, give from your heart because you want to give, not because you have to or are forced to give. Your reward will be greater when it comes from your heart not because you want something in return.

Author and entrepreneur, **Mark Albion** remarks, *"We get so busy with our stuff, it's easy to forget others' needs, and our affect on them."*

It's so true. Life is hectic but we can't use that as an excuse. No amount of money or objects should come between us and caring for others.

Abigail Van Buren, the Dear Abby columnist says, *"There are two kinds of people in this world – those who walk into a room and say 'Here I am' and those who say 'There you are."*

Which one are you?

We all know the old saying, **"Do unto others as you would have them do unto you,"** but how many of us actually follow that type of reciprocity? We run around all day trying to get things accomplished but the idea of chasing the wrong things works against us. You end up not giving yourself a chance to do the right things.

When we put things ahead of others we allow them to rule our every thought, feelings, and choices. The all encompassing drive to have more money, more power, and more stuff is a never ending search in vain. What happens is we become desperate and unhappy. Our life becomes a virtual prison and we can't escape it.

Did you know that for the majority of people, one specific action of helping others provides a greater deal of personal joy and satisfaction that any amount of money can ever provide? It's something they cannot replace by material items. Helping others often requires no financial resources and can create good karma for everyone involved.

One of the big ideas being taught by the self-help gurus today involves loving ourselves. So much emphasis is being placed on loving ourselves that we forget that we need to love others just as much. In the wide scope of things, it is in the way we feel about ourselves that affects the way we treat others so the only way to create love in your life is to share it with others.

Try making people around you feel happy and it will help you feel happy. Money can't buy you love (thank you Beatles) and it can actually alienate you from the ones you love. The honest thankfulness you get from others will increase your self-esteem and what's more, those that you treat well will likely repay you with the same kindness when you really need it.

A word of caution; don't use the idea of putting others first as a means to let people walk all over you. Be strong in character, honest in your dealings, and humble in your actions.

WHEN LOVE AND MONEY DON'T MIX

"You look at your bank account, and you see the currency of love and happiness is more important than the currency of money."
—Richie Sambora

According to **Sara Konrath, Ph. D.**, a psychologist and faculty member of the University of Michigan, a study was led by **Dr. Suzanne Richards** from the University of Exeter Medical School. **Dr. Richards** reviewed more than 40 studies done over the past 20 years regarding the link between volunteering and one's overall health. The study found that people who volunteer have lower instances of depression, have an increase in their overall well-being, and a 22% reduction in the risk of dying prematurely.

They found that if you want to live a longer, happier, and healthier life, get out and volunteer with those in need. It's much healthier for both you and the other person involved.

The idea of giving of yourself instead of just money seems to echo with the deeper part of our souls. It's not just about the money but the actual giving that brings about real love.

It's nice to have money but material possessions don't mean a thing, especially when you lose someone close to you. Money can't bring them back.

My wife comes from a poor family in the Philippines but money was never the most important thing in their lives. The idea of God and family always came first. When her parents both died from long illnesses, it wasn't the money but the love they shared which she will always remember.

We are born naked and die naked and when we look back on our lives, what kind of legacy did we leave? Were we selfish with our things? Did we share our time, our talents, and our treasures with humanity? Or did we run a long and lonely race acquiring objects? Sharing of ourselves with others is one of the greatest gifts of love we can ever provide.

When you cultivate a healthy relationship with money and use it in a way that makes everyone happy… that is when you experience true harmony in your life. We all love having money in our bank accounts but if you base your life on happiness and loving others, the money will come, it just won't be your guiding force.

According to **Frederic Koenig**, true wealth is this: *"We tend to forget that happiness doesn't come as a result of getting something we don't have, but rather of recognizing and appreciating what we do have."*

When you regard money as the backbone of your self esteem, you find out what really matters. When your ideas about money clash with your belief system, a disconnect occurs. You either pick money or happiness… you can't have both.

Learn from the mistakes **Ebenezer Scrooge** endured in **"A Christmas Carol"** by **Charles Dickens**. Scrooge's lust for money eclipsed his ability to love others and made him into a miserly old man with no friends. Only after being shown what his life was like by the ghosts of Christmas past, Christmas present, and Christmas future did he realize the folly of his ways. He goes on to share his entire wealth with the poor and learns a valuable lesson about money.

On his Facebook page dated January 19, 2012, bestselling author **Robert Kiyosaki** talked about money and happiness this way; *"Change your focus, from making money to serving more people. Serving more people makes the money come in."*

You see, when you concentrate on others, you will get what is coming to you. Those that live a life of love reap the benefits. Those that put money first are doomed to a life of loneliness and unhappiness. It has been shown time after time after time that the key to becoming wealthy both in mind, body, and your wallet, comes from sharing of yourself… anything else is a bonus!

DISCOVER THE SHEER
POWER OF PRAYER

"Faith makes all things possible... love makes all things easy."
—Dwight L. Moody

W hat is prayer and how does it help us to show love in a world that seems so filled with hate?

According to author **Robert Velarde**, *"Prayer is a relationship, wherein we humbly communicate, worship, and sincerely seek God's face, knowing that He hears us, loves us and will respond, though not always in a manner we may expect or desire. Prayer can encompass confession, praise, adoration, supplication, intercession and more."*

Prayer is the ultimate concept in adding love to our lives. When we give of ourselves to God, we are able to give to others. Prayer helps us to unlock the true self and see God for what he has done for us.

Why do we need to pray?

Once again **Robert Velarde** unlocks the key to God's love in prayer. *"Because prayer is the means God has ordained for some things to happen. Prayer, for instance, helps others know the love of Jesus. Prayer can clear human obstacles out of the way in order for God to work. It is not that God can't work without our prayers, but that He has established prayer as part of His plan for accomplishing His will in this world."*

Finally, he says that *"Prayer keeps us humble before God."* Humility is the essence of love. When we put others ahead of ourselves we are actually fulfilling the prayers that God asks us to pray for. This love binds us all together as humanity. When we pray for love, God opens the doors of opportunity for us to not only share in his love but the love of others.

The power of prayer does not come from our end but from God Himself! When we ask according to the will of God, we are certain he hears us. Whatever it is we want, it must conform to His will. It is a leap of faith that changes our life forever. In **Daniel 11:32**, it states: **"...but the people who know their God will display strength and take action."**

God takes action on our prayers because He loves us. Without prayer we cannot access the power of God.

SHOULD WE PRAY FOR OTHERS?

"Prayer becomes more meaningful as we counsel with the Lord in all of our doings, as we express heartfelt gratitude, and as we pray for others."
—David A. Bednar

W e are commanded by God to pray for others. In fact, we should be praying for our enemies as well. In **Matthew 5:43-44**, it is written, ***"You have heard that it was said, "Love your neighbor and hate your enemy." But I tell you: Love your enemies and pray for those who persecute you ... "***

Though we naturally feel like we shouldn't pray for our enemies, in order to imitate Christ's love, we need to grow in maturity to enable us to actually love and pray for our enemies.

This is what sets us apart from others and what gives us that chance to heal our lives. Praying for others shows how unselfish we are and when we put the emphasis on others God helps heal the problem areas in our own lives.

We all have problems that make life hard for us but if you think you can overcome them on your own you are barking up the wrong tree. Without the power of God securely behind us that small stone we push through life becomes a huge boulder we cannot hope to move.

Francis Chan, the best-selling author of the books "**Crazy Love**", "**Forgotten God**", "**Erasing Hell**", and "**Multiply**", writes, *"Prayer is a way of walking in love."* This is a beautiful way to explain how important prayer is to the act of loving others.

To understand how prayer reshapes our brains, **Dr. Andrew Newberg, MD**, Director of Research at the Myrna Brind Center for Integrative Medicine at Thomson Jefferson University Hospital and Medical College, has attempted to see how the spiritual experience we feel when we pray changes the brain and bodies of people who feel connected with God.

This new field is called **"Neurotheology,"** and they have found that people who spend hours praying and in meditation have changes in their brains which are far different from non-praying people.

Those prayers lead to a sense of oneness with the universe and blurred the boundary between one's self and others. It is in this oneness where the love that is all around can change us. Scientists have also found that we can change our brains for the better through prayer and meditation.

When we believe our prayers can make a difference it changes who we are. We start living a life centered more on loving others than ourselves. This, in turn, begins a transformation in us where God takes over and brings us closer to him. The closer we are to Him the better our lives can be. The more blessings God will pour out to us and the easier it will be to handle the problems we encounter along the way.

A September 9, 2014 article written by **Traci Pederson**, entitled, **"Praying To A Loving God Guards Against Anxiety Disorders,"** she states that *"Prayer not only changes who we are but it also changes us physically. Researchers from Baylor University found that people who pray to a loving and protective God are less likely to experience anxiety-related disorders - worry, fear, self-consciousness, social anxiety and obsessive compulsive behavior - compared to people who pray but don't really expect to receive any comfort or protection from God."*

The Baylor Religion study which is entitled **"Prayer, Attachment to God, and Symptoms of Anxiety-Related Disorders Among U.S. Adults,"** was first published in the journal, "**Sociology of Religion**" and found that the 1714 volunteers who participated had much lower instances of general anxiety, social anxiety, obsession, and compulsion.

Researcher **Matt Bradshaw, PhD** remarked that *"God is a source of comfort and strength and through prayer they enter into an intimate relationship with Him and begin to feel a secure attachment. When this is the case, prayer offers emotional comfort, resulting in fewer symptoms of anxiety disorders."*

For me, God was my source of comfort and helped me become the person I am today. Without His help I would still be suffering from all the emotional problems I had before. He helped me change my heart and learn to cope. Once I could cope with all my anxieties, I could open my heart to experience the love that God had for me.

Traci continues with, *"The findings add to the growing body of research confirming a connection between a person's perceived relationship with God and mental and physical health."*

An online **Columbia University** study published on Dec. 25, 2013, revealed that 103 adults who had a high risk of depression (based on family history) were asked how important praying and spirituality played in their everyday lives.

The research was led by **Lisa Miller**, a professor and director of Clinical Psychology and director of the Spirituality Mind Body Institute at Teachers College, Columbia University. When the team studied the brain MRI's of the adults, they found those who those who regularly practiced meditation and prayer had thicker parts of the brain's cortex than those who didn't pray.

According to **Lisa**, *"The new study links this extremely large protective benefit of spirituality or religion to previous studies which identified large expanses of cortical thinning in specific regions of the brain in adult offspring of families at high risk for major depression."*

It doesn't matter what religion you belong to, prayer has a calming effect on your psyche. I know how important it has been for me.

But it's not just the big things that have helped me see the love that God has for me. No, I see it every day in the little things. I see it in my children, my friends, and I see it in everyone I meet. Love is so potent that I can't help but see what love can do.

When you understand how important prayer is and the connection it has with loving others you will see how much of an impact it can have on your own life.

Here's a great example of how prayer works in the real world.

Five year old **Josiah Duncan** and his mother were about to order breakfast from an Alabama Waffle House in early May of 2015 when the boy saw a disheveled man come and sit down in a corner by himself. When he pestered his mom to find out why no one waited on the man, his mother explained he was homeless and didn't have the money to buy food.

The little boy asked his mother if they could buy the man breakfast and she obliged. He walked over to the homeless man and asked him what he wanted to eat. The man asked for some bacon but before he could eat, Josiah led a prayer with the man along with the eleven others in the restaurant. According to CNN, Josiah started to sing: *"God our Father, God our Father, we thank you, we thank you, for our many blessings, for our many blessings, amen, amen."*

The boy's unselfish act of love brought the entire restaurant to tears. His mother was so proud of him and remarked, *"You never know who the angel on Earth is, and when the opportunity comes you should never walk away from it. Watching my son touch the 11 people in that Waffle House tonight will be forever one of the greatest accomplishments as a parent I'll ever get to witness."*

It doesn't matter if you have never prayed before, what is important is that you start right now. Give yourself a chance at experiencing the love that God offers. He will change your life, your circumstances, and you will receive the rich blessings that He has promised you.

THE UNBREAKABLE LINK
BETWEEN PRAYER AND LOVE

"Never forget the three powerful resources you always have available to you: love, prayer, and forgiveness."
—H. Jackson Brown, Jr.

ere's what **Mother Teresa of Calcutta** had to say about prayer and love.

"Everything is there: God, myself, and my neighbor. If I forgive, I can be holy, I can pray. Everything comes from a humble heart; when we have such a heart, we will know how to love God, how to love ourselves, and how to love our neighbor (Mt 22:37). That is nothing complicated, and yet we complicate our lives so much and make them heavy with so many extra loads. Only one thing counts: to be humble and to pray. The more you pray, the better you will pray."

To me, my growth in loving others has all been predicated on my prayer life. Even when I feel overwhelmed and exhausted from physical pain, I know and feel the love Jesus has for me and it makes all things bearable.

124

To those who scoff at the connection between prayer and love are missing the whole point of what makes prayer so special. It is to humble ourselves before God and bask in the love that He has for us. When we experience his divine grace it makes it that much easier to go out and show that love to others.

I remember all the prayers that have been answered and I feel blessed to be a part of that love.

In January of 2001, my wife found out she was pregnant and we were both thrilled. We already had a boy and a girl and were looking forward to another bundle of joy in which we could show our love to but it wasn't meant to be. Just a few weeks later, my wife had a miscarriage but it wasn't just any type of miscarriage.

My wife was sick in bed for a week after finding the miscarriage but I knew something was seriously wrong with her even though she told me she was fine.

I was at work on a Saturday morning and tried to reach her by phone all day but to no avail. At that time, my son was turning seven in a few weeks and my daughter was just two and a half. As with any mother juggling a job and two young children, I knew it was getting tough for her to cope. My intuition told me to get home right away.

I told my boss I needed to go home ASAP as I felt something was definitely wrong with my wife. When I got home, I found her unconscious on the bed while my kids were sleeping in their rooms across the hall. I tried to revive her but she wouldn't wake up. I was frantic. I called my parents to come and help me with the kids as I took care of my wife. She finally awoke but was groggy and totally out of it. My parents arrived within fifteen minutes to take my kids while I whisked her off to the hospital emergency room.

The assessment: An ectopic pregnancy… which in layman's terms means the egg grew in her fallopian tube and not in the womb. When it got to be too big, her tube burst and the baby died. My wife on the other hand, unknowingly was slowing bleeding to death on the inside. The doctors told me had I not brought her to the hospital when I did, she would have died within the hour.

But that wasn't the worst of it. She underwent four and a half hours of emergency surgery in which they cleaned out all the blood that had seeped into her stomach and sewed up the fallopian tube as well as some other medical procedures (I'm not a doctor so I'm not quite sure what else they actually did) to stabilize her condition.

The doctor's weren't sure they could save her because her blood pressure had dropped so much and she barely had a pulse but for those four and a half hours I prayed more fervently than I had ever prayed before.

My prayers were answered and my wife survived. In fact, our prayers were answered once again by a loving God two years later when my youngest daughter was born. The doctor's flat out told us that since my wife was pushing forty years old, had only one functioning fallopian tube and had been through major surgery on her reproductive system to try and save her life, the odds were astronomical that she could even conceive again. But at age forty one, she held our beautiful daughter in her arms in the hospital bed and that tiny little beautiful baby girl brought our family even closer together.

Think of all the times in your life when things seemed hopeless but they worked out. Who do you think was watching over you?

I find it puzzling that people will brush these incidents off as coincidence but when it happens to them they are the first to pray even though they don't believe.

It goes to show you that when you pray, pray for those things that involve love for not only yourself but your family, friends and those people who really need your prayers.

An answered prayer is a physical illustration of God's love for us so keep on praying to be loved as well as to love others.

LOVE AND MEDITATION

"Meditation is the life of the soul: Action, the soul of meditation; and honor the reward of action."
—Francis Quarles

How can meditation help us love to others?

Meditation is a way of transforming our hearts and minds with practices and techniques that encourage and develop a keen awareness of our concentration, our clarity, our emotional makeup as well as an inner calmness that helps us see the true nature of things.

Without understanding and seeing this true nature, we are like a muscle that never develops. This development helps build up our awareness to see others in a new light. It is a beautiful light that shines without hesitation and without any prejudice whatsoever.

Love does not need to have its own light but it is a light that shines around us. We, as humans, have built walls around ourselves and never allow anyone to see the real person inside. Meditation is used to break those barriers and help us grow the love we have with gentleness and caring that attracts others to us.

Meditation is a way of calming our spirit and seeing the goodness we have inside and then helping it come forward with the grace of God's love. There is nothing we can do without God's help.

When we are troubled or in pain, God is there to ease and care for us like the loving Father He is. With meditation, I was able to see God's love in a brand new light. My prayers were more God-centered instead of only on me and I saw myself as our Lord sees me - a person that is loved and cared for. That was so important to me. Before, I had always felt alone but now I had Jesus in my corner and I knew I could accomplish anything I put my mind to as long as it was what he wants me to do.

In his biography, **Steve Jobs** talked about how he used meditation to calm his mind and unleash his creativity.

"If you just sit and observe, you will see how restless your mind is ... If you try to calm it, it only makes things worse, but over time it does calm, and when it does, there's room to hear more subtle things - that's when your intuition starts to blossom and you start to see things more clearly and be in the present more. Your mind just slows down, and you see a tremendous expanse in the moment. You see so much more than you could see before. It's a discipline, you have to practice it."

A loving and kind heart is at the center of a person who is at one with God. According to Buddhists beliefs, *"Hatred cannot coexist with loving-kindness, and dissipates if supplanted with thoughts based on loving-kindness."*

That loving kindness starts within and works its way outward. Meditation is a way of sending loving kindness towards others. With meditation, we can arouse our feelings of loving kindness in a variety of ways.

Here Are 4 Powerful Ways To Make Meditation Work For You

1. **Visualize loving another person** - No matter who it is, see yourself being joyous and loving towards another human being. They could be family, friends, coworkers or even a total stranger. The idea is to visualize a strong enough emotional love so that you send positive energy their way.

2. **Reflect on the love of others** - By reflecting on other's positive qualities we can send loving kindness everywhere. Reflect on the goodness you see in them and help magnify it in them.

3. **Spend quality time alone in prayer** - Send out love vibrations to God. Allow Him to strengthen your resolve to be kind to others. Let Him show you where you must concentrate your energy on and watch as your life changes for the better.

4. **Use breathing techniques to calm your mind** - Get in touch with your inner spirit. Find a place where you can recharge your spirit and focus positive energy in your life.

These types of meditation work very well in helping us to be aware of the love that is around us. We don't need anyone to help us to meditate in this fashion. It is for self-awareness and for helping us to project goodness into this world,

Meditation centers us and strengthens our love for others. It is a calming influence in our lives that breeds contentment and patience. That patience is sorely lacking in contemporary living and meditation brings it to the forefront of life.

I have found that meditation is a way to help the flow of love that I know I have inside of me come forward in a very peaceful way. With all the distractions of daily life and the problems that we all face, meditation is a way to recharge our batteries and get us in touch with a higher place.

Meditation and prayer can be used together to fashion a more caring attitude and one centered on the true love of God. If we give ourselves the chance to be free of all the hate we have built up inside, our hearts can then focus on purity of love.

You will never know what true happiness is until you can free yourself of hate and anger. I know it's hard to do and most of us feel it's a place we will never see but it is in the journey that we hope to achieve a lasting peace. Even with all the pain in my life I have been able to do it so I'm telling you through experience that it is possible.

One byproduct of meditation is a strong and keen awareness of your thoughts. The more negative thoughts you employ the more negative you will act. Meditation is tool that is used to bring more love into our lives by replacing the negative aspects with the positive vibrations.

Studies have shown that those who meditate are much happier than those who don't. The reason behind this is quite simple; meditation works with those areas of the brain that are used for happiness. The more we access those areas the more happiness we bring into our lives.

Meditation is just another way we can bring more love into our lives. Use it for your own happiness and the happiness of others.

Why Is Meditation So Important To Healing Your Mind?

According to **Rebecca Gladding M.D.**, *"Meditation changes our perspective on life. Our minds start thinking differently about things. "In the end, this means that you are able to see yourself and everyone around you from a clearer perspective, while simultaneously being more present, compassionate and empathetic with people no matter the situation. With time and practice, people do truly become calmer, have a greater capacity for empathy and find they tend to respond in" a more balanced way to things, people or events in their lives."*

This is so important to healing our lives. When you are able to bring peace to your mind, to your heart, and to your life, wonderful things start happening. You can deal with life in a more positive manner, you don't let the little things bother you as much, and you can enjoy life with a deeper appreciation of all it has to offer.

Meditation increases your life energy and who couldn't use more energy in their life? That high octane energy is like a vacuum that clears out the emotional pollution you have stored up inside your mind all these years.

Using the proper meditational breathing techniques floods your body with the healing power of oxygen. Every cell is bursting with new life. Those negative emotions that were always bombarding your mind are flushed out and replaced with a calming spirit.

Finally, the tensions, anger, and frustrations that made your life unbearable are released and your mind is free to explore the power of positive energy you can give back to the world.

Is this really possible?

According to neuropsychologist, **Rick Hanson**, founder of the **Wellspring Institute for Neuroscience and Contemplative Wisdom** and author of *"Buddha's Brain: The Practical Neuroscience of Happiness, Love, and Wisdom," "The mind takes the shape of whatever it rests upon. If you routinely rest your mind on self-criticism, anger, or anxious rumination, your mind will take a negative shape."*

This is why meditation fundamentally retrains your brain to release its inner fears, anxieties, and negative emotions. Your mind then becomes less stressed out and better able to deal with life from a clearer perspective. Those old thoughts and emotions cannot actively shape your brain any longer.

Meditation is the calming effect that helped me transform my life from worrying about everything, being negative, and scared to becoming confident in my abilities, learning to love others and to trust in God. Don't underestimate its power within you and how it can change your own life. You will see a much happier and much loving you in time.

STEP 3

MAKING LOVE WORK

BE AN INSPIRATION
TO THOSE AROUND YOU

*"In a full heart there is room for everything,
and in an empty heart there is room for nothing."*
—Antonio Porchia

Have you ever been inspired to do something special in your life? Have you ever been inspired by others to make a difference in the world?

To inspire someone can be an incredibly significant accomplishment, especially if it makes a difference in that person's life.

Inspiration is powerful in its own right but it isn't easy to do. You need to build lasting relationships with people and become a positive influence on them. How you deal with others determines the extent of your influence.

Traci Porterfield, the founder and CEO of **Love by Design**, a personalized matchmaking and relationship coaching service, says that people look for certain qualities in others who inspire them. ***"Although we are often deluded into***

135

searching outside of ourselves for these qualities, in reality, everything we are seeking is within. Conditioned beliefs may obscure our experience of our essential nature, yet we can rediscover our innate state of love and happiness by taking small and intentional steps."

American novelist **Stephen Chbosky** *puts our feelings about love in perspective by saying,* **"We accept the love we think we deserve."**

If this is true then we need to understand that inspiring others is a great way to add more love into our life.

To be an effective leader for God, you need to learn how to inspire others in a way that shows how much you care. We all know sharing is caring and to be able to share your love is something most people don't expect when talking about inspiration.

Do you want to inspire others?

Before we can inspire others we must first understand what true inspiration actually is.

WHAT IS INSPIRATION?

"True inspiration overrides all fears. When you are inspired, you enter a trance state and can accomplish things that you may never have felt capable of doing."
—Bernie Siegel

efore I answer this question, let me say that everyone can and is inspired during their lives yet they feel it is something they don't possess. I hear people say all the time, ***"I'm not a creative person so how can I get inspired?"***

It's not about just being inspired but awakening the spirit to tap into the love that is all around you. From there, inspiration is freedom. The freedom to understand what is important in our hearts and being active participants in allowing that inspiration to work in our lives.

How often have you felt lonely and uninspired? Those are the times when we feel we are loved the least. To harness the power of inspiration we need to overcome obstacles that hinder our attempts to love.

Some of these may be self-doubt, anger, physical, mental and/or emotional pain that is blocking our chances at inviting love into our hearts.

I went to the Merriam-Webster dictionary to find out what the definition of inspiration is.

Here's what I found.

1. something that makes someone want to do something or that gives someone an idea about what to do or create: a force or influence that inspires someone
2. a person, place, experience, etc., that makes someone want to do or create something
3. a good idea

I believe inspiration is a divine process that stimulates our creative nature and brings out our imagination, our inner genius, and the power within. This power is the act of aligning yourself with the full abundance of life. It is a believing that anything is possible.

The source of inspiration is always there. According to **Trevor Hill**, a life coach from England, *"Inspiration is an all-embracing experience. It has a major influence on how we interact with the world."*

How do you interact with others?

Is there inspiration that connects you to the outside world?

He goes on to say that inspiration gives us a sense of well-being, helps unlock our hidden gifts and most importantly, it helps us enhance our relationships.

For those of us who are shy (like me), learning how to become an inspired person is the key to helping us get along with others. I find myself being inspired all the time because I open myself up to being inspired by what others do. It's through that inspiration that I am able to give more of myself to others.

How Does God Inspire Us?

We are inspired through God's guidance. He guides us through our circumstances and we can either make the most of what we are given or complain about everything. Most people do the latter and lose all hope for God's guidance.

Throughout my life, I thought I could handle everything but when it got too much for me to handle, I finally gave up and realized it was God's guidance I needed.

Life is like that. We need others to help us get by only in my case it took a near-fatal car accident to seek divine inspiration.

Inspiration comes from a place of deep love. A place many of us don't visit quite enough.

We are told to be a light unto others but through this light we must learn how to first notice life from a different view. We need to explore and find our inspiration in the little things.

John Stilgoe is a professor of the history of landscape at Harvard and says *"Exploration happens best by accident, not by following a schedule."*

The idea that inspiration comes solely from perspiration isn't quite true. God has given us so much to be inspired by and to use to inspire others. We just have to open our hearts and let God work in our lives to see inspiration take root.

HOW TO INSPIRE OTHERS

"I testify that inspiration can be the spring for every person's hope, guidance, and strength. It is one of the magnified treasures of life. It involves coming to the infinite knowledge of God."
—James E. Faust

I nspiration is hope.

Hope for a future filled with love and guidance from God. Hope for faith that guides our every move. Hope for a love that brings us the strength to do magnificent things with our lives. Finally, a hope that we don't compromise and live a life less than what we deserve. That's what inspiration does for us.

Here Are 9 Strategies You Need To Learn To Become An Inspiration To Others

1. **Earn people's trust** – Trust is something you build up over time, not something that comes right away. This is why it is so important to treat others with love and respect from the start because trust can be destroyed in an instant and then you are no good to anyone. People watch what

you do and say and if you are not someone they can emulate, you lose your effectiveness.

2. **Be a positive influence** – If you are not a positive person, how can you be a positive influence on others? Our attitudes play a big part in how we support and encourage others. Those that look to you for guidance need to know you are a positive person and live in a positive manner. Success breeds success through imitation and when you are positive, others can build off of that.

3. **Learn how to build up people's confidence** – When you offer compliments that build up people's confidence, you inspire them to take positive steps in their own lives. People always want to be around someone who makes them feel good but make sure you are honest in your compliments. Don't be nice for the sake of being nice. Make it count. Making people feel good is a great way to inspire them to take on challenges. Share your experiences, your struggles, and your story to encourage others in their own walk. This is a great way to build up a community.

4. **Acknowledge other's contributions** – None of us can do everything on our own. We need others to bounce questions off of, help with completing a project, or even to get feedback. When you acknowledge other's contributions, it show's them you are humble enough to give proper credit due for everything they do. This also builds trust. Don't underestimate the trust factor when you acknowledge others contributions. It brings people together much quicker.

5. **Give good and honest advice** – The mark of true love is giving advice that is not only good but is truly honest. No one likes to be lied to or be given advice that is too vague. Your honest critique allows other's to hone in what they need to do to better their lives. People trust honest advice as long as it doesn't hurt one's feelings. That is counter-productive. The same goes for giving advice if you don't know what you're talking about. If you can't help, find someone who can. They will appreciate your help even more, will respect your honesty, and be thankful for you caring enough to find the answer that is needed.

6. **Accept your own flaws but show confidence** –We all have flaws. The key here is to focus on being confident instead of hiding our flaws. We don't want to be over critical of ourselves to the point where we show a

lack of confidence. People want to be around confident individuals not stuck-up or phony types that don't inspire that confidence. This also means you should be sharing your failures as well as you successes so that people can relate to your experiences.

Showing you're your human side will help others appreciate the real you. Remember to use your flaws as a teaching device not as a put down on yourself. You want to inspire confidence not have people laugh or feel sorry for you behind your back. You will easily lose their confidence that way.

7. **Be enthusiastic in everything you do** – Your enthusiasm is contagious to everyone around you. Your positive energy can inspire great things in others and leads to much better communication with everyone involved. Enthusiasm though, is nothing without the right ideas that work. Just rushing into something with all-out enthusiasm doesn't work if you fall flat on your face. Instead, make sure you have all the information you need to make good, solid decisions.

    You also need to make sure you pursue alternative ideas from others and see their side of the equation. You'll inspire trust in others who might otherwise not want to approach you because they may feel you are too firm in your convictions and not flexible enough to incorporate other's ideas.

8. **Be a good communicator** – Communication is probably the biggest contributor to being an inspiration to others. When you say what you mean and follow up with it, people know they can trust what you say.

    Learn to use the right words to inspire confidence. You don't need an amazing vocabulary, you just need to be able to look others in the eye, talk with authority, and say what needs to be said. People are more apt to accept what you are saying when you say it with confidence. But beware of the phrase, *"Fake it till you make it."* People can see right through that.

    Being a good communicator also means watching your own actions. How you act is just as important as what you say. Your actions can push others away if you are not a humble person. We have all had that boss who was arrogant and pushy. Don't be that kind of person.

9. **Share your life's experiences** – Share your wisdom and knowledge so that others can benefit. The more you can be a resource that helps

others grow the better you can be at inspiring others. You may feel you don't have anything to share but each one of us has experiences, gifts, and know-how that can positively enhance another person's walk through life

Have you noticed how all these skills I have shown you are skills that successful people have? These types of skills are born out of love. A love for others that shows in everything they do.

I encourage you to start changing how you act towards your fellow man by incorporating these skills into your personality. They will make you a better person and someone others will look up to.

By learning these skills you will become the person you were meant to be. But remember, you must take action. Everything you do must be proactive. Wanting to change your circumstances, your heart, and your mind takes work but it is in the learning that you become transformed.

Today, every part of our actions are scrutinized. Social media is an incredibly powerful force and our lives and reputation can be shattered in an instant. This is why it is so important to be an authentic and genuine person. Let your actions speak for themselves. It's not about your place in society but building up society as a whole so that we all benefit.

Show real love to everyone you meet, treat others as you would have them treat you, and live a life that rises above the pettiness of everyday life. Only then you will be able to inspire others.

Don't worry what others think, instead, be pleasing to the Lord and you will be pleasing to others. Of course, we will never please everyone so concentrate on doing what is right even if everyone thinks you are wrong.

So many people miss this part and think they cannot inspire others so they give up before they even try. What you need to find is the proper motivation.

HOW TO MOTIVATE OTHERS

"Motivation is what gets you started. Habit is what keeps you going."
—Jim Ryun

The next part of inspiration is based on how much you can motivate others. Without motivation, inspiration falls way short.

To be a good motivator you need particular skills that can bring out the best in others. Motivation is all about getting people to do things that they may not want to do but is right for them so that's where you come in. You have to win their cooperation and that is done with love and care.

Growing as a person involves learning how to overcome the many pitfalls that come your way but becoming a success means being able to take that knowledge and motivate people to become better themselves.

Here Are 4 Ways You Can Be A Great Motivator:

1. **Share in everyone's sacrifice** – If people don't see that you are invested in their outcome they won't follow you. Show them you are willing to get your hands dirty for their benefit.

2. **Get people to take action** – Your enthusiasm and trust in someone's abilities means more to that person than words could ever say. People will take action and direction from you when you do it out of love instead of forcing them into it.

3. **Focus on people's emotions** – We, as humans are ruled by our emotions. To motivate people, we must make a personal connection that focuses squarely on that person. It's all about being honest and authentic in how you relate to that person. When you show genuine love and care, it's easier to get others motivated.

4. **Lead by example** – We are called in the bible to lead by example. We find it in **1 Timothy 4:12**. *"Let no one despise your youth; instead, you should be an example to the believers in speech, in conduct, in love, in faith, in purity."*

Leading by example is a perfect way to show others that you walk the walk and talk the talk. People will follow you when you take the lead.

Motivation is all about the people you're working with or spend time with. Those that give of themselves become the best motivators.

We should all strive to be a positive influence on humanity and the more we can inspire and motivate people, the more we can tap into the love we all have inside.

There are so many facets to love that it may seem overwhelming to live a life filled with love but I never said it would be easy. Each day is a new day to work on a particular aspect. You will have every opportunity to practice them in your dealings with people on a daily basis. Don't let those opportunities go by. Instead, embrace them and latch on to the power they offer.

CULTIVATE COMPASSION
IN YOUR LIFE

"If you want others to be happy, practice compassion.
If you want to be happy, practice compassion."
—Dalai Lama

The act of compassion is not something we do for good deeds or when we feel bad for someone else's plight. In fact, it goes much deeper than that. Compassion rises out of the need for us to help others through a sense of shared suffering.

We've all been hurt before, had painful moments in our past, and have even been devastated by a calamitous event but it is in that shared suffering where we need to take concrete action.

I have seen my share of thoughtless people who ignore those in need and it shocks me to the core how uncaring some people can be. The greatest example of compassion I have ever seen comes from the life of **Mother Theresa**. She lived a life based on total compassion for her fellow man, serving people who were neglected by the rest of humanity.

To her, compassion was based solely on the idea of God's love. The type of love that few of us have the courage to put into practice nor the heart to endure. I think this quote by her expresses the incredible amount of love she had for the all the suffering in this world.

"Let us touch the dying, the poor, the lonely and the unwanted according to the graces we have received and let us not be ashamed or slow to do the humble work."

When she was awarded the Nobel Peace Prize in 1979, she described what her mission in life consisted of: *"To care for the hungry, the naked, the homeless, the crippled, the blind, the lepers, all those people who feel unwanted, unloved, uncared for throughout society, people that have become a burden to the society and are shunned by everyone."*

At one time, I felt exactly like those people she talks about. I felt shunned, unwanted, and saw myself as a burden on society but it took a gift of God to turn my life around.

Mother Theresa was a great human being who we should all strive to be like in our daily life. Of course, for many of us, we fall very short with our own compassion, allowing our selfish concerns to rule over our hearts and minds but that doesn't matter. It is in the attempt to better other's lives that we find the strength to be compassionate.

Here is what she asked us to do. *"Let no one ever come to you without leaving better and happier. Be the living expression of God's kindness: kindness in your face, kindness in your eyes, kindness in your smile."*

This is what I have learned from her; always make sure the person you deal with leaves a better person after they meet you. Sometimes we fail but it is in our pursuit of changing people's lives that we create real love.

In **Mathew25:31-46,** Jesus instructs us as to what compassion is all about. It's a long verse but it shows us how we are to treat others

"When the Son of Man comes in his glory, and all the angels with him, he will sit on his glorious throne. All the nations will be gathered before him, and he will separate the people one from another as a shepherd separates the sheep from the goats. He will put the sheep on his right and the goats on his left.

"Then the King will say to those on his right, "Come, you who are blessed by my Father; take your inheritance, the kingdom prepared for you since the creation of the world. For I was hungry and you gave me something to eat, I was thirsty and you gave me something to drink, I was a stranger and you

invited me in, I needed clothes and you clothed me, I was sick and you looked after me, I was in prison and you came to visit me."

"Then the righteous will answer him, 'Lord, when did we see you hungry and feed you, or thirsty and give you something to drink? When did we see you a stranger and invite you in, or needing clothes and clothe you? When did we see you sick or in prison and go to visit you?"

"The King will reply, 'Truly I tell you, whatever you did for one of the least of these brothers and sisters of mine, you did for me.'

"Then he will say to those on his left, 'Depart from me, you who are cursed, into the eternal fire prepared for the devil and his angels. For I was hungry and you gave me nothing to eat, I was thirsty and you gave me nothing to drink, I was a stranger and you did not invite me in, I needed clothes and you did not clothe me, I was sick and in prison and you did not look after me.'

"They also will answer, "Lord, when did we see you hungry or thirsty or a stranger or needing clothes or sick or in prison, and did not help you?'

"He will reply, Truly I tell you, whatever you did not do for one of the least of these, you did not do for me.

"Then they will go away to eternal punishment, but the righteous to eternal life."

When you love others, you will see the opportunities to do for the least of mankind. It does not need to be hard. You can start right now. You can become a compassionate person and change not only your life but the lives of countless others if you humble yourself and decide to choose a life based on pure unconditional love.

In order to be a compassionate person, you must first embrace compassion as you would any other habit. It must be with you everywhere you go, in everything you do, and with everyone you meet. It cannot take days off, sleep in when you're too tired, or be a reaction to outside stimulation. Instead, it must be an action first and foremost where you take the initiative. The act of compassion is a way of life not just a way of thinking.

The **Dalai Lama** says we should meditate upon it every day and put it into practice so that it becomes an integral part of our daily life. We must develop an appreciative heart for everything around us for without appreciation we cannot be compassionate.

I can hear people saying, *"That's all good and fine but what about the real world? It's not all about happy thoughts and goodwill toward others you know.* " Point well taken but therein lies the conundrum. If you don't change your thoughts and habits, you will always lack true compassion.

Growing up as a child, my mother raised me to aware of other's suffering but I never really grasped the concept of what true compassion was until I saw life in the poorest parts of the Philippines.

Like so many others before me, I used to disassociate myself from my emotions and turn away when I saw suffering, hoping that out of site would lead to out of mind but being in the Philippines changed all that.

I was never really "poor" by their standards but I suffered greatly with my own inner demons. I didn't realize how good I had it until I met people who looked at me as if I was a millionaire and saw only the good in me. It was a rude awakening and one that forced me to confront my greatest fears.

After my car accident, I saw a different side to life. A side that allowed me to live… a side that allowed me to understand what real compassion was.

If so many people were being compassionate towards me and my problems, how was I to react, or in this case, take action?

I began studying how others practiced compassion and saw a pattern develop. I wanted to emulate them… but how?

How would a shy, selfish person like me, who had no real confidence in himself, no money, and not many friends turn his life around and reach his full potential?

Easy! I saw compassion as a way to fulfill my destiny in life and place the emphasis on others instead of myself. I saw myself serving others and being an inspiration to them in my thoughts, my deeds, and especially my words. I made it a point to see the good in others. Though I struggled at first, my strength comes directly from the Lord.

True compassion comes from unconditional love. You don't ask for anything in return, you just give of yourself and let it end with that. It is an act of unselfishness that is pure in its decisions and humble in its service.

EMANATING KINDNESS
AND COMPASSION

*"True compassion means not only feeling another's
pain but also being moved to help relieve it."*
—Daniel Goleman

Where would compassion be without kindness? Kindness is at the root of all forms of compassion. No matter what we do or where we go, kindness should be the driving force in how we treat others. I'm not talking about the forced kindness that everyone tries to pass off to be known as a **"good person."** I'm talking about a kindness that comes from deep within the soul... the type of kindness that instantly draws people to you and builds lasting bridges of love.

Kindness can be likened to an electrical current that constantly emanates from each one of us and turns on the light of love between humans. When you break the bonds of kindness, you break that flow of energy and cause pain... pain for the other person and as well as for yourself.

The **Dalai Lama** says, *"My message is the practice of compassion, love and kindness. These things are very useful in our daily life, and also for the whole of human society as these practices can be very important."*

Have you ever heard the phrase *"Pay it forward?"* The idea behind this is to show kindness to other people when they are in need.

A great example of this happened when a hidden camera was set up in a **Mattson's Family Market** in Burlington Township, New Jersey for a segment called **"What Would You Do"** on the ABC television show **20/20**.

They hired actresses to play customers who couldn't pay for their food purchases. In each case, the actress had to decide between getting rid of certain food items (usually baby food or a staple food) and finding a way to pay for their purchase with money they didn't have.

The customers waiting in line behind them didn't know they were being filmed and unselfishly reached out to the woman and gave her money to pay for the food she couldn't afford. It happened time and time again. Their unselfish acts showed true compassion.

They think first of their neighbor before their own needs. In the program, one of the customers said all that needed to be said with this quote. *"If you can help somebody else, do it!"* And another customer who also gave money, chimed in, *"It doesn't matter who you are or who I am, we're here to make a difference."*

The money they gave they needed to pay for their own food but helping someone who really needed it was far more important to them. This is what I'm trying to get across to you. When you offer acts of genuine kindness to others, you tap into the love that is all around and then pass it on. Don't just think about it… do it!

WHY SELF-COMPASSION LEADS
TO COMPASSION FOR OTHERS

*"Feeling compassion for ourselves in no way releases us from
responsibility for our actions. Rather, it releases us from the self-hatred
that prevents us from responding to our life with clarity and balance."*
—Tara Brach

B efore we can have compassion for others we must first have compassion
and respect for ourselves. We need to understand our own suffering
and use that to help others. Remember, small acts of compassion are an
opportunity to interconnect with others in an empathetic nature.

Each one of us must be in harmony with our own brand of compassion.
Even though you cannot run out of compassion, you must balance how you treat
yourself with how you treat others.

When we're conflicted with problems or stress we tend to internalize these
things and they keep us from becoming the kind of compassionate person we

want to be. We worry about our own problems and don't see how others are struggling with their own difficulties.

When we find a balance between our own struggles and those of others, we make acts of compassion a powerful reality.

From the "Journal of Clinical Psychology: In Session", August 2013, they examine self-compassion and offer this diagnosis, *"Common humanity involves recognizing that the human condition is imperfect, and that we are not alone in our suffering. Often, however, we feel isolated and cut off from others when considering our struggles and failures, irrationally feeling that it's only "ME" who is having such a hard time of it. We think that somehow we are abnormal, that something has gone wrong. This sort of tunnel vision makes us feel alone and isolated, making our suffering even worse. We forget that failure and imperfection actually are normal."*

That's where I went wrong. I thought there was something wrong with me but I realized we are all the same. We share the same goals in life, the same feelings, and the same suffering. It's all in how we deal with our problems that makes the real difference.

They go on to write, *"With self-compassion, however, we take the stance of a compassionate "other" toward ourselves, allowing us to adopt a broader perspective on ourselves and our lives. By remembering the shared human experience, we feel less isolated when we are in pain."*

It is in this isolation that we lose our compassion for own circumstances. Finally, the article states that *"suffering becomes the "connective tissue" that unites us to others."* Take that suffering you feel and use it to bring joy to others and in that single act of compassion you will also bring joy to thy self.

Too many of us wallow in self-pity and isolate ourselves from life instead of sharing the good we have with others. When you share of yourself, you share the goodness that is the sweet spot for love.

You don't have to be alone anymore. I used to feel that way but it has all changed. I can now see others in a more positive light. I don't compare myself to others… instead, I see how much we all have in common and I use that to offer help to those that need it. Love has opened my eyes to the validity of who I am and how much I can share with others.

If you share the commitment to give of yourself you will have compassion for both your own struggles and those people you come in contact with everyday.

WHAT ARE THE
HEALTH BENEFITS OF COMPASSION?

*"The purpose of human life is to serve, and
to show compassion and the will to help others."*
—Albert Schweitzer

B eing kind and compassionate is just as good for you as the person you are
helping. There are numerous studies done that show he physical benefits
to practicing a life filled with compassion.

1. **DHEA** is a natural hormone made by the body which counteracts the
    aging process and stops cortisol, which is known as "stress hormone."
    Those that practice being kind and giving compassion produce 100%
    more than people who don't. If you want to bring more happiness into
    your life, start being more compassionate.

2. According to **Emma Seppala Ph.D.**, The National Institute of Health
    released a brain imaging study where they found that the pleasure centers

of the brain are activated when we see money going to a charity as much as when it comes back to us.

3. Compassion is an uplifting experience. **Jonathon Haidt** at the University of Virginia found that when people see others showing compassion, it physically lifts our spirits and makes us happy.

4. Compassion is a mood enhancer. It can reverse feelings of anxiety and depression and shifts the focus where it should be… on others.

5. It's a natural health booster. Studies have shown that those who practice compassion have better physical, mental, emotional, and spiritual health in their lives and are far more resistant to the affects of illness on their bodies.

6. **Elizabeth W. Dunn**, a professor at the University of British Columbia and **Michael I. Norton**, a professor at the Harvard Business School, write that people who spend money on others tend to be happier than when they spend it on themselves. This was taken from an article entitled, **"Spending Money on Others Promotes Happiness"** in Science magazine dated March 21, 2008.

As you can see, practicing compassion leads directly to better health and that is a great byproduct of love. The more genuine the compassion and empathy you feel for others, the more love will come back to you.

FINDING PEACE IN A
WORLD FULL OF HATE

*"Balance, peace, and joy are the fruit of a successful life. It starts with
recognizing your talents and finding ways to serve others by using them."*
—Thomas Kinkade

Peace is a word that is talked about much but rarely practiced. We all want it in our lives but in a world full of hate, it takes a very strong (both emotional and physical) person to overcome life's obstacles to find that elusive peace.

Peace is not just about what we find at the end of the journey but the journey itself. It may come with broken promises and bouts of anger as well as good intentions but that should not derail you with your goal of finding and giving love.

To find peace, know that you are the driver but to access that peace you must first come before God. There is only one place you can find that peace and God is the answer.

Inner peace is all part of love's journey and when you make the attempt to bring peace into the world it should be for unselfish reasons.

Peace is His condition. It is a way of living but unless we have a firm foundation, peace is but a pipe dream. No one knows what the future may hold so peace of mind depends on trusting in God. Our Lord knows what is right for us and it is His peace we are looking for.

From his book, "**Finding Peace**", author **Jean Vanier** makes this observation about gaining peace in our lives. *"When we love and respect people, revealing to them their value, they can begin to come out from behind the walls that protect them."*

Gaining this peace brings people together. He goes on to say, *"Peace is the fruit of love, a love that is also justice. But to grow in love requires work - hard work. And it can bring pain because it implies loss - loss of the certitudes, comforts, and hurts that shelter and define us."*

Throughout our lives we look for things that make us happy. Some people search forever for happiness through sex, drugs, and alcohol but it's an empty feeling. Inner peace comes from God's eternal and unconditional love and when we are able to share that love, we share in the happiness as well.

God needs to be central to our lives. There is no peace or even hope apart from knowing him. In **Philippians 4: 6-9**, it is written:

"Do not be anxious about anything, but in everything, by prayer and petition, with thanksgiving, present your requests to God. And the peace of God, which transcends all understanding, will guard your hearts and minds in Christ Jesus. Finally brothers, whatever is true, whatever is noble, whatever is right, whatever is pure, whatever is lovely, whatever is admirable - if anything is excellent or praiseworthy - think about such things, Whatever you have learned or received or heard from me, or seen in me - put it into practice. And the God of peace will be with you.

When you read those words, you understand it's the peace of God that sticks to your hearts and minds to carry you forward.

How do you get that peace?

7 Ways To Access Your Inner Peace

1. **Live by faith** - The spirit will empower you to live a life filled with love. As stated in **Hebrews 11:1** *"Faith is the assurance of things hoped for,*

the conviction of things not seen." Faith is something you can't see or feel. You have to believe it's real and allow it to become part of you.

2. **Trust the Lord** - Without that trust, there is no peace. God's faithfulness is everlasting. He will not let you down. Trust is a big word which most people are afraid of. If you believe in the power of God and know he is the Lord... that he died for your sins and loves you more than you can ever imagine, why sweat the small things?

3. **Do not worry** - Tomorrow will take care of itself. Allow the peace of God to strengthen and guard your mind because he cares about you. Our minds have been set free from slavery so don't let worry occupy part of your mind that can be used to experience the great things of today. Don't try to fix things you have no control over, just work on those things you can make a difference in both yours and other people's lives.

4. **Practice what you were meant to do** - Pray, meditate on the word of God, and do what God calls you to do. You were put here in this world because God has a vision for you. Be who you are and celebrate that. God loves you so much and wants you to be happy but if you try to be someone you are not, you're cheating the world out of experiencing the real you.

5. **Live in the world of today** - It is our inability to let go of the past that robs us of being at peace with ourselves. We want to change the past so badly that we keep its memory alive even though there is nothing physically, mentally, or emotionally we can do to go back and fix things and make them right.

   Why do you want to hold on things that cause you pain and suffering when there's a whole world in front of you to find peace and happiness? We will never know what the Lord has in store for us unless we give him the chance to mold us into the loving people he wants us to be.

6. **Learn to accept things for what they are** - I know there are many things I'd like to change about myself but I can't have everything so I have accepted them for what they are. I can write songs but I'm not a very good singer. Even though I love to sing I will never be a professional. I've accepted that but it doesn't mean I will give up singing. It just means I know my limitations.

The same goes for you. Know your limitations and be happy with them but change the things you can change. We're never happy with how things are right now so we do everything we can to change them but in the end, resistance is futile. Short people want to be taller, tall people want to be shorter, those with curly hair want straight hair and those with straight hair want curly hair. The list goes on and on.

We all want something we cannot have yet we never seem to embrace those qualities that are right in front of us such as those qualities that others find so remarkable in us but we tend to overlook while searching for things that don't really matter.

If I could go back in time, there are many things I would have changed about myself but I know I can't so I file them away and move on. Those memories are too painful to remember and I don't want to suffer from them anymore. I stopped fighting with myself a long time ago and so should you.

7. **Start spreading peace outward** - Spread your joy and love outward and they will radiate among others which opens up waves of serenity. Peace is not a one way street. It doesn't start and stop with you. Share it with others and it will come in droves back to you.

We all have a war going on inside of us but we have the power to end that war. **Pema Chodron**, an ordained Buddhist nun and acclaimed author of **"When Things Fall Apart"** writes, *"If we want to make peace with ourselves and with the world at large, we have to look closely at the source of all our wars."*

Whatever war you have going on in your mind is painful. I understand your pain but it's something you can overcome if you are willing to fight. Fight for your right to be happy and for your right to live a life full of meaning.

Allowing the Lord to dwell in your heart is the only way to find true peace. That peace leads to loving others in a way that everyone wants to be a part of. When you eliminate hate and anger from your heart, you have the peace of the Lord. What can be better than that?

LIFE FROM THE HEART

"A heart is not judged by how much you love,
but by how much you are loved by others."
—Frank Morgan

W e have come to the final part of our training and it's time to put everything you have learned into practice. We all want to be loved and the more we love the happier we will be.

Knowledge without action yields no fruit that is why it is time to get out there and start loving your fellow man. A subtle shift in your mindset is actually all it takes to put everything into practice.

Instead of looking at the differences we all have, start by focusing on the commonalities we all share. Each one of us is searching for happiness in our life so be a moment of happiness in one other's life.

It's time to live in the here and now! To be with others you can share the joy of life with. Below is a quote that spurred me on to changing my mindset and living from the heart.

"Life is Love, enjoy it; Life is Challenge, meet it;
Life is a Song, sing it; Life is a Dream, realize it;
Life is a Game, play it; Life is a Goal, achieve it."
—**Sathya Sai Baba**

Life Is Love

We live but do not fully love. Do you understand how profound that statement is? Too many people are just existing and not enjoying the full measure of God's love.

They work hard but gain nothing from it. They try but do not succeed. They live on autopilot without feeling the world around them. Every part of life is love whether it makes you happy or sad.

This is where balance comes in to play. Change your mindset and see everything as love and you will enjoy life as if it were blood flowing through your veins. See life… live life… be a part of life. God has given it to you as a special gift so make love your life.

Life is Challenge

Each day gives us a new chance to meet the challenges in our lives. God tells us in **Matthew 6:26:** *"Look at the birds of the air; they do not sow or reap or store away in barns, and yet your heavenly Father feeds them. Are you not much more valuable than they?"*

If we are so valuable to God then why must you run and hide? Why must you live in sadness" God has fed you with His unconditional love and when you spread that love around you will have the power to meet those challenges.

For years, I couldn't see myself ever being happy or living in abundance but when I changed my heart and let Jesus take over the steering wheel, I not only met my challenges but I thrived in spite of them. That's where living from the heart instead of your pocketbook or wants and needs gives you the upper-hand.

Life is a Song

How often do you sing? I mean, how often do you have a song in your heart? When you are happy you sing but what if you aren't feeling so great? Can you still sing?

Jesus answers that with this convincing verse from **Psalm 34:17-20**

When the righteous cry for help, the Lord hears and delivers them out of all their troubles. The Lord is near to the brokenhearted and saves the crushed

in spirit. Many are the afflictions of the righteous, but the Lord delivers him out of them all. He keeps all his bones; not one of them is broken.

Live with a song in your heart for the Lord will always be there for you. When you are bitter, lift up that bitterness up to the Lord, when you are sad, lift up the sadness to the Lord, and when you feel you cannot go on, lift up your burden to the Lord and allow His song to play in your heart.

The reason why I believe is because it worked for me. If I can find a beautiful song in my heart then Jesus can change yours and help you find the song that changes yours.

Life is a Dream

We all have our one special dream we want to accomplish in our lives but it can seem overwhelming to achieve. According to **Pastor Rick Warren**, "*The first thing God does to build your faith is give you a dream. When God wants to work in your life, he'll always gives you a dream - about yourself, about what he wants you to do, about how he's going to use your life to impact the world.*

When you put your faith in God he will reward your dreams but you must be an action taker. You can't sit on the sidelines and hope you'll get what you need. God wants you to go out and do His will on Earth. **Pastor Rick** goes on to say, "*God starts with a dream as he works within your life to build faith.*"

Your faith brings your dream to fruition and brings glory to God.

Life is a Game

As the lottery is famous for saying, "*You gotta be in it to win it,*" it's a message we all need to follow. Too many people see life as a game they cannot win but it's not in the winning that brings us happiness but in the playing that rewards God's followers.

Life is a struggle for everyone whether you are rich or poor but God sees above those things. He has given you everything you need to be successful but you must make the commitment to Him to access the fruits of the Holy Spirit.

Play your life as if God depends on it because it does. Only then will you find true peace, lasting love, and unequaled happiness through the healing of our Holy Father who loves you more than you could ever fathom!

Life is a Goal

Do you know why you were put here on this Earth?

You were made for something great and beautiful. Your goal is to love and be loved. Everything else comes from those two things. Without them you have nothing.

I see people everyday struggle to come to terms with their lot in life. They complain about it, wallow in it, and do nothing about it. **Tony Robbins**, the great motivational speaker and self-help genius tells us to do this and we will see change: ***"The state you are in determines your abilities. Everyone's got the ability. It's like I have a great computer but if I'm not going to plug it in, I am not going to have much power,"***

That great computer is God. Plug in and get ready to realize your goals!

Here Are 5 Steps To Begin Living From The Heart

You don't just start living from the heart and expect to realize all your amazing dreams. You need to start changing how to look at the world, how the world looks back at you, your mindset and what your thoughts consist of as well as how you act. These five steps are the basis for change. Learn them… Use them… and live by them!

1. **Smile** - This may sound ridiculously easy but you'd be surprised at how many people don't smile. I see far too many frowns on my daily journeys. A smile really does brighten a person's day but it can also make it much easier to break down barriers we all put up while approaching others. A smile is a positive action that instills trust while a frown automatically sends out depressing emotions.

2. **Be positive and act positively** - Have you ever been around people who bring you down? It's not the best of experiences. These types of people bring everyone down no matter where they are. Even if I'm feeling a bit depressed or don't feel well, I still try to be positive around others. I try to have a positive impact on other people's lives wherever I go no matter how I feel. The people who have made the biggest impact on my life were the ones who were both positive and uplifting. Those are the people I gravitate to. Which one do you want to be?

3. **Learn people's names** - You have a much better chance at making a great impression on someone if you remember their name. It makes them feel special and you can then make a real connection.

    I've always been bad with names. No matter how hard I tried I'd forget people's names… especially at the wrong time. Studies have shown that hearing the sound of one's name activates our brain, even when it's spoken in a room that's cluttered with noise.

I've learned a neat little trick that can help you overcome this and connect you with people on a much deeper level. When someone introduces themselves to you, automatically say their name out loud while greeting them and connect their name to a famous person. The next time you see them, the image of the celebrity will be fresh in your mind.

When I meet someone wearing a name tag, such as a store employee or at an event, I always greet them by their name. Once again, it puts them at ease and makes them feel special. You never know how much you can change a person's outlook when you make them feel special.

4. **Look for ways to help others** - Don't wait to be asked. Go out of your comfort zone and offer help to someone who needs it. Practice the art of kindness. Make everything you do special and involve others in making it special. This could be sharing jokes, your tim, or even preparing food for someone who is hungry. The more you practice helping others the more opportunities you will have to receive love in return.

5. **Connect with people** - Not just your family or inner circle of friends but people in general. Go out of your way to be nice to people you've never met. Talk to people. Find out what you can do to improve their lives. Remember, we are not islands unto ourselves who only care about what's important to us. If you go through life only worrying about what you are doing you will never invite enough love into your life to make a real difference.

Have you ever met a person who has such a zeal for life? Everything they do seems to have a magic about it. Ever wonder how they do it? The secret lies in living their life to the fullest and not just existing. They involve others in their fun, give more than they receive, and take an interest in the people around them.

I used to be so involved with my own personal problems that I would give lame excuses to myself as to why I didn't get involved with others. Things such as, *"Well, I'm too shy"* or *"I don't have the time or any money"* were my mantras. It seemed I gave any old excuse not to deal with others. I had distanced myself so much I didn't know how to offer love without being scared they wouldn't return the favor so I stopped myself before I had a chance to find out.

I've been hurt too many times in my life which has made me gun shy. I missed out on life and all the love that was out there. My experiences were few and far between as I let my anger, my hate, and my frustrations rule my life. It wasn't until I started putting others first that things changed for me.

Today, I live my life with a grateful heart. It doesn't matter what others think of me (I can't change anyone else but myself so I don't even try), it's what I can do for others that really counts. Having been given another chance, life is precious to me. Not just mine but everyone's.

Whenever there's a chance to make a difference in my daily dealings I take the initiative. I choose honesty, humility, and love as a means to create a legacy for myself. I don't want to die knowing I didn't love more than I received.

I use these five basic functions to create opportunities to live from the heart and they will work just as well for you… but you must use them or healing cannot begin.

LIVING A LIFE FROM THE HEART

"Live your life from your heart. Share from your heart.
And your story will touch and heal people's souls."
—Melody Beattie

A ccording to **Dr. Gail Brenner**, *"When you live from the heart, you begin to touch into the universal experience of love. Love is the source of everything - the fabric which makes up our very existence."* It's in this universal experience that we can share our love. She finishes by saying, *"In any moment you have a choice - the head or the heart, inauthenticity or truth, distraction or love. Play around with living more in your heart. Don't be shy. Let love in, and life's greatest treasures will be revealed."*

Living a life from the heart means having a loving and gentle heart. A gentle heart does not mean a meek heart. It is a caring way of going about your business that makes everyone feel better about themselves.

When we choose to contribute to other's lives it makes us feel worthy to be loved. It gives us the confidence to be who we were meant to be. Living from the heart takes courage. It means trusting in the Lord and living and loving with our whole heart.

Ask yourself these 4 important questions

1. What can I give to others in any given situation?
2. How will my life have mattered when I die?
3. What is the greatest gift I can offer this world?
4. What can I share that will make a difference in other people's lives?

Humans tend to get into daily habits that are hard to shake but if you can start the habit of living in the present, you can experience life in all its beauty. The world is a beautiful place if you let yourself become part of it. That's where your happiness lies.

Bestselling author **Kristine Carlson** examines living from the heart by saying, *"Remember to live this moment and each day as if it could be your last and you will experience greater joy and deeper fulfillment. Let go of your fears and be here now. In this moment all is well and you can be at your very best."*

To be your best is to open your heart to the goodness that life has to offer. To see it, touch it, and smell it reminds us of the very essence and beauty of life.

Can you change the world with your heart?

I believe you can but I'm not the only one. Christian Ministers **Yael and Doug Powell** had this to say about the heart: *"Your heart truly can change the world! When your heart is open and you feel love, your heart pulls your brain and all of your bodily systems into harmony with it. This creates clear thinking, intuition, health and inner peace."*

Following what is in your heart is one of the keys to living a fulfilling life.

Here Are 7 Things You Can Do To Live A Fulfilling Life.

1. **1: Trust in your heart** - Everything we are comes from our heart. It is where God lives within us and sets us apart from the rest of the world. Trusting your heart means trusting God.
2. **Free your mind of clutter** - One of the most important things you can do is remove the useless clutter from your mind as well as your life. Do things that are important and leave the worries to God. The more you worry, the less time you have to live in the moment. Each day you must

take out the garbage from your mind before it starts overflowing and stinking up your life.

3. **Align your heart with God's will** - This may well be the most important thing you can ever do! We all have free will but when we can align them with what God wants for us we experience a much deeper sense of love and happiness. We live as God wants us to live and see God in everything and everyone.

4. **Be an authentic person** - Being your own person and being true to your own beliefs is what makes an authentic person. Don't worry about being different. It's knowing your heart is true and living God's will to the fullest. Being genuine means having self respect and the respect of others while remaining natural in your approach to life. The real you must come across every time and with everyone or you run the risk of losing trust with others.

5. **Share your heart** - Sharing what you have with others is the mark of an unselfish person. It should never matter how much you have but how much you give. I have known so many people who basically have nothing but they give because it's who they are. The bible says this about giving in **Hebrews 13:16,** *"Do not neglect to do good and to share what you have, for such sacrifices are pleasing to God."* The gift of you is what people want. This includes your personality, your quirks, even your vulnerability. It's what makes you, you. That's all anyone expects and needs.

6. **Become an example of peace and love** - Most people only talk a good game about peace and love but those who actually live in the trenches are the ones who make a difference in the world. Action always speaks louder than words and when you are an example of peace and love, many blessings will come your way.

Bestselling author and humorist, **Erma Bombeck** gives us some great advice regarding what we should be doing with our lives. *"When I stand before God at the end of my life, I would hope that I would not have a single bit of talent left, and could say, "I used everything you gave me."*

The end of your life should be a treasure trove of memories and the love you shared is your ultimate gift to others. Give everything you have and you will be pleasing to God.

HOW TO LOVE OTHERS WHEN I DON'T EVEN LOVE MYSELF?

"If you can learn to love yourself and all the flaws, you can love other people so much better. And that makes you so happy."
—Kristin Chenoweth

L ook, we've all made mistakes in our lives. I'm no different but the past is the past. It cannot be changed and you cannot get it back. Instead, learn from your past and use it to inspire your quest to learn the ways of love.

Here Is My 12 Step Approach To Make The Most Of Loving Yourself

1. **Accept yourself -** When you accept yourself for who you are, you melt most of the emotional bondage you've put yourself through. You then begin the healing process. Strive to be the best you can be and accept what happens. Remember, acceptance does not mean defeat, it means loving who you are.

In this quote from **Sanaya Roman** and **Duane Packer**, we see what we're capable of when we accept ourselves. *"Don't discard your fantasies as merely wishful thinking. Honor them as messages from the deepest part of your being about what you can do and directions you can choose."*

2. **Be yourself** - You are a unique individual who has been put on this earth for a reason. You have the right to love yourself. Too often we compare ourselves to others and believe we are not as good as them. Forget that kind of thinking. Instead, bask in your own uniqueness and be the beautiful person God made.

3. **Be honest with yourself** - There are times and places where you have failed but also where you have succeeded. You are not perfect but it's in the quest to be a better person that we live a life based on love. You are not as bad as you think or as great as you want to believe. It's somewhere in between and that is where balance is achieved. Remember, you are a child of God and you are loved. That is where you should focus your life on.

4. **Don't take life for granted** - If you take your relationships with others for granted you will be let down more often than not. This is a recipe for pain and pain leads to self-loathing. That self-loathing is a hard nut to crack. Appreciate what you have and what you are. Without having some type of appreciation you have no solid foundation to stand upon. Take each day as it comes and appreciate what you are experiencing now for it will be gone in time.

5. **Live in the now** - Throughout this book I have been telling you to accept the past but live in the present. The present is all you have and that is what you should focus on. Your happiness depends on today not what happened yesterday. Don't let the past stop you from enjoying the present and rob you of what you can accomplish today.

6. **Let God's love guide you** - This means responding to each situation in a loving and peaceful manner. This reduces stress and helps you tap into the energy of love. Of course, you will need to address your fears and habits but that is what love is for... guiding you on your journey in life. You are going to make mistakes, but with love you can give of yourself and know you did your best.

7. **Practice empathy** - Empathy allows you to see others in a caring and loving way. Tap into that empathy regarding yourself and you will see things are not quite as bad as you think. In fact, you might just embrace those experiences as a teaching moment. Empathy is also a great trigger for releasing self-blame. Whether it was your fault or not, give yourself a break. Don't wallow in the pain of past mistakes. Move on to bigger and better things.

8. **Make peace with yourself** - Stop fighting a war within yourself and realize there is no winner and no loser... just the beautiful person God made. When you come to a place of peace, you can release the love that's deep within your heart.

9. **Stop stressing over being perfect** - I hate to be the bearer of bad news but you will never be perfect. It is not humanly possible but God has made you perfect in His image. Don't compare yourself to everyone else and their situation. Instead, focus on becoming the best you possible. It's those imperfections that make you unique.

10. **Foster stronger relationships with others** - The more we are loved by others the more we can start loving ourselves. The bonds of friendship strengthen our happiness which leads to greater self-awareness. This is the ideal setting for bringing out the love we all have inside. Friendships are great for reinforcing the bonds of love. Sharing love helps you become more aware of your own goodness.

11. **Learn how to express your emotions in a caring and constructive way** - If you suppress your emotions you are bound to live with the pain you've experienced. Instead, give yourself the right to experience your true feelings. Your emotions are good things. Learn to express them in a way that oozes love and kindness... not anger and hate. This way, you control those times when negative emotions start to rile up inside. Don't beat yourself up for being emotional. See those emotions as signs of being human and as moments to bring love to the forefront and express the goodness you have inside.

12. **Stay away from negative people** - Negativity is one of love's greatest enemies. The more we are around negative and uncaring people the more we take on their qualities. Even if you have been friends with people like this for a long time, it's best that you break those bonds of friendship for your own sake. Just imagine what it would feel like if you were only

surrounded by positive and uplifting people? Wouldn't you be a much happier and healthy individual?

Love is a very complicated subject. There's no manual that teaches us how to love but the idea is to engage the people you come in contact with and be a beacon of hope to them. For that, you were made to love!

SHOWING UNCONDITIONAL
LOVE FOR OTHERS

*"The greatest gift that you can give to others
is the gift of unconditional love and acceptance."*
—Brian Tracy

I t goes without saying that the key to real happiness is to love and be loved in return. Without love we have nothing to live for nor do we have anything to offer of value. Life would be pretty awful if there was no love in the world but since that isn't the case let's find some ways we can show our love that will make a big difference in other people's lives

Blogger **Kris Karr** put love this way, *"Show your love courageously. Show your love openly. Show your love with no strings attached."*

If we aren't open to showing our love then how can anyone see the love we have to share? Sometimes, you just have to throw caution to the wind and take a chance on people.

It can be difficult to tell others how we are feeling inside because when we put emotions out into the world, we know we can get hurt. Sharing that love means you are willing to put your heart on the line and are not expecting anything in return.

You don't even need to state your love in an open manner. There are so many ways to share your love. Praying for others is a great way to send positive energy. Instead of email, texting or sending a tweet, call someone on the phone and talk to them. This is a great way to open up and give of yourself, especially if it's someone you haven't spoken to in a while. Just hearing your voice can be a ray of sunshine to someone who may be wondering how you are doing.

Showing our love to others can be hard to practice if we feel we've never had anyone show us love. Unconditional love is something talked about in great deal but many people are unfamiliar with what it actually is. They think it gives them a license to do what they want because the other person will always love them but it doesn't quite work that way. Unconditional love does not come easy. It is something we must learn how to do and practice all the time.

Here is a quote from **Chris Moore** which pretty well sums up what unconditional love is. *"Love is to love someone for who they are, who they were, and who they will be."*

We must give away our love for it to be unconditional. There should be neither strings attached nor expectations of any kind. Whether we succeed or fail at loving unconditionally is of no consequence. It is in the practice of caring and doing for others that we get our reward.

Despite our trying to love unconditionally, it is through God's unconditional love that we have a perfect example of how we should offer ourselves to others. Too many times we feel we are not worthy enough to show unconditional love to make a real impact in other's lives

When Jesus died on the cross, it was the greatest act of unconditional love ever known. Giving his life for our sins gives us the roadmap for putting unconditional love into practice.

In his book, "**Unconditional Love - Radical Stories Real People**", author **Ben Stroud** puts this type of love into perspective.

"Unconditional love heals the broken, empowers the timid, affirms the hesitant, and elevates those who have been overlooked, forgotten, and silenced. There is a power that comes to those who show and to those who receive unconditional love. Those who show this love are released from being consumed

with themselves. Those who receive this love are released from limitations others have placed on them."

Each of us has the capacity to love. How much we give and how much we receive is all based on what limits we put on ourselves. In an article by **Lissa Rankin** dated February 14, 2012 entitled, **"How To Love Unconditionally & Still Stay Sane,"** she says this about unconditional love. *"Unconditional love is epic. You can't earn it. You don't get to choose who receives it. It goes beyond all logic and exceeds your ability to understand it. It just is."*

Don't think about how to give love, just give it! Don't waste precious time with things you can't change. Life is to be lived and practiced. There is so much love out there waiting to be experienced. Be the one that gives it first!

In her book, **"Personal Prayer Through Awareness"**, author **Sonaya Roman**, writes that unconditional love, *"Is learning to be the source of love rather than waiting for others to be the source."*

The whole idea behind living a life based on love is the humility of being unselfish. Yes, you may get hurt but don't let that stop you. It's all part of the learning process. If we are the source then love comes to us as we give it out. It is the **"Circle of Love"** and we need to practice living in this circle.

If you wait for love to show it may never come. When you are the source of love you become the glue that sticks to everyone else.

Sonaya goes on to say, *"You learn to love by putting yourself in situations that challenge you to be loving."* If we don't challenge ourselves, we will never know true love.

Life is a big challenge but it's not about winning or losing but getting into the game and experiencing it.

Too often I watched others living while I sat in the bleachers. It was both humiliating, and boring, and something I will never do again.

God has given you this life. What are you going to do with with it?

EMBRACING JOY

*"Focus on the journey, not the destination. Joy is
found not in finishing an activity but in doing it."*
—Greg Anderson

T o embrace joy is to open ourselves up to being hurt. It is very important
to remember to receive joy in an appreciated way. When we feel that
joy we have an innate sense of being whole. Embrace that sense. Feel it!
Surround yourself with it. Bask in it.

Live in the moment of joy. Cherish the idea that you are loved. It's a great
feeling when you are wanted and people include you in their lives.

You can give that same feeling to others when you include them in your life.
The idea that we have to always be in a state of joy in order to give love is not
healthy. If you go looking for love you may not find it but if you go out and give
love joy will find you.

If you come from a place that is full of confusion and darkness, the idea
of feeling joy may overwhelm you. You don't have to jump right in. Wet your

feet first and bask in the joy that others are sending you and when you see an opportunity to give joy back then jump in and make it a worthwhile endeavor.

This is where joy comes in. Being joyful is to experience a profound sense of love. Joy is a happiness that comes from deep within our souls. Have you ever experienced this type of deep joy?

Earlier, I talked about love being the current that runs through each one of us and if it is cut off then love cannot flow through us. That type of love comes from emanating joy. The joy you send out to the universe you will get back tenfold. Joy is the love you feel that is blessed by God. This joy is transformational. It brings about a change in both how we act and in the people we share joy with.

Finding joy can be very a challenging subject especially if you are you afraid to love with abandonment. Experiencing past hurts may keep us from knowing joy but joy is a beautiful feeling to behold. Fully expressing it is something you may not be accustomed to. We all suffer from suppressing our true selves at times and withholding our natural feelings but without finding joy we cannot embrace love.

As I was growing up, my father didn't know how to express his feelings. He hid behind behaviors that limited his capacity to show love. To him, showing love was a weakness and he didn't want to appear weak in front of me.

I desired love from my parents but I never fully experienced the true joy of that love. Coming from a broken home meant I would have to receive love when I could get it not when I wanted it. That was very painful! The joy I did receive was fleeting. It could never live up to what I had envisioned in my heart and mind.

Accepting God's grace is the path to embracing joy. If I know that God loves me then I can love others through the joy of His grace.

Peter Kreeft, Ph.D., a professor of philosophy at Boston College says this about joy, *"Joy is more than happiness, just as happiness is more than pleasure. Pleasure is in the body. Happiness is in the mind and feelings. Joy is deep within the heart, the spirit, the center of the self."*

That is so powerful. Joy is not just happiness but an extension of God's love that He has given to each one of us!

He goes on to say that, *"Most deeply, everyone wants joy"*

Of course everyone wants to find joy but we are all looking in the wrong place. We substitute joy for feeling good or satisfying ourselves with ungodly pleasures but the only way to satisfy that craving is through the love of God.

Peter finishes by saying, *"In the very act of self-surrender to God there is joy. Not just later, as a consequence but right then."*

We fill our lives with material goods that don't give us joy and then we feel lost and lonely. The Greek word for joy is chara. It is related to charis which means grace. God's grace is the joy we look forward to when we yield to his spirit.

Joy grows out of our faith, our gratitude, our hope, and especially our love. It is the second fruit of the Holy Spirit. In **Galatians 5:22-23** it states, *"But the fruit of the spirit is love, joy, peace, forbearance, goodness, faithfulness, gentleness, and self-control. Against such things there is no law."*

The road to joy is paved with the love of God. It is a beautiful gift but sin can rob us of that joy. My road to love goes through the Lord but it wasn't always that way. My sin got in the way of me experiencing joy. I was stubborn in my ways and it took a near-fatal car accident to get my attention.

Do I have your attention yet?

Happiness can be fleeting but to rejoice in the Lord is forever. Learning to be joyful comes with a warning though. It is not easy to be joyful as we must endure trials in our lives and our faith will be tested. With God's help, we persevere through these trials which bring about a true joy and contentment.

We may not appreciate those things that may be taken away from us yet we go on because we trust in the Lord. True joy is ever eternal as it is based on our relationship with the Lord who brings us peace and joy.

Peace and joy are responsible for loving others in a way that strengthens the bonds between people. My love for others brings me closer to them in a way that I can share my joy.

Embrace joy and be willing to share it. **Thich Nhat Hanh**, the Vietnamese Buddhist monk and author puts joy in perspective by saying, *"Sometimes your joy is the source of your smile, but sometimes your smile is the source of your joy."*

Finding joy amidst trials can be tough but it is learning from your trials and knowing that God is with us. He gives you that ultimate joy and the strength to endure everything.

If I am to love others I have a great example to live by. God asks us to embrace his love and through this love we are to pass it on. I am passing my love on to you. Take it and then pay it forward. Don't think about it or even try to understand it. Instead, give it back freely and pray that what you have done will help someone along their own journey through life.

HOW TO REAP WHAT YOU SOW

*"The law of harvest is to reap more than what you so.
Sow an act, and you reap a habit. Sow a habit and you
reap a character. Sow a character and you reap a destiny"*
—James Allen

L ife is a harvest. Our lives are spent working towards a common goal and
how we spent our days and nights directly affects who we are.

Are you planting kindness in your life?

Are you sowing an attitude that is giving in nature?

What we give in this life we will receive in return. If you are kind to others
they will repay you with kindness. If you sow anger and hate, your life will be
filled with anger and hate. You have the choice. You have free will to do what you
want but isn't it better to be good in God's eyes?

The famous author **Robert Louis Stevenson** once remarked, ***"Don't judge a
day by the harvest you reap but by the seeds that you plant."*** Those good seeds

will grow abundantly and be multiplied by God. When you give like God he will help you reap a tremendous harvest in your life.

When I was at my lowest point, I was living what I had sowed earlier in my life. I was so unhappy with my job, my finances, and my failures that I spent too much time trying to help myself and not enough time helping others. I was so fixated on my own problems that my happiness was based on my own sense of imperfections. It wasn't until I started giving of myself and cultivated kindness and compassion did I receive it in return. I wasted so many years feeling sorry for myself.

Is your life a barren field made up of dying seeds? If so, try focusing on what you have and not on what you lack and be generous with what you do have. Plant good seeds and watch them grow. Your harvest will be bountiful and your happiness will be unending.

The bible is clear on this in **2 Corinthians 9:6-7** where **God** states: *"Remember this: Whoever sows sparingly will also reap sparingly, and whoever sows generously will also reap generously. Each of you should give what you have decided in your heart to give, not reluctantly or under compulsion, for God loves a cheerful giver."*

What is your life like right now? Are you filled with happiness, kindness and generosity or do you think you can be a better person? Be honest with yourself. The principle of sowing and reaping applies to every facet of your life.

This idea of sowing and reaping is an important lesson when it comes to dealing with people. I'm a shy person by nature and try to be good to others but I find it hard to approach people. I hid behind my shyness and have used it as an excuse. Only now have I come out of my shell and pushed myself to put others first. It is a learning process but one I know I should have learned much earlier.

My actions have consequences and so do my words. For every action I undertake I reap what I have sown. Those consequences may not show up right away but the effects will be apparent in time.

The idea is to sow your time, your talents, and your treasures for the good of the community. Your community will be better off because of your unselfishness and your rewards will be greater in God's eyes. What you do, do it in the name of honesty and love and you will reap great rewards.

What character traits do you have distilled in your heart? How can you use them to better the lives of others? So many of us go through life building up treasures that we cannot take with us but don't realize it until it's way too late. Don't be that person. Don't wait until it's too late!

In Tagalog, the national language of the Philippines, they use a word called *"pakikisama"* which means getting along with others but in its deepest sense, it means the sharing of one's wealth, talent, time, and self with others. It is so ingrained in their DNA that it's how they live. It's about helping one another to get along in life, to care for one another, and to help their fellow human beings when they're in need. To act in this manner is to reap what you have sown.

It is in the serving of others that we sow the seeds of love. For it is in serving others that we serve Christ. The Christian life is one of servicing others, showing love and kindness to everyone, even those who may not treat us very well. We should ensure we use every opportunity to serve others.

True service is all about improving the lives of everyone around us in an unselfish way. **Anne Frank** said it best: *"How wonderful it is that nobody need wait a single moment before starting to improve the world."*

Serving God is the greatest form of charity and when we serve others we show our love of God. It is the simple acts of kindness that show our love for others and those acts are not forgotten by our Lord. He sees and knows what we do. We need to be reminded that loving other people isn't optional; it is a command by Jesus himself!

We should heed the advice of **John Wesley** when he says: *"Do all the good you can, by all the means you can, in all the ways you can, in all the places you can, at all the times you can, to all the people you can, as long as you can."*

Serving others is a pure expression of your love. Anyone who possesses that love for God will perform acts of loving service for others. You can't fake that kind of love. It has to come from the heart. When you do this you will reap the true benefits of God's unconditional love.

HOW TO USE VIBRATION, BALANCE
AND HARMONY TO DISTRIBUTE LOVE

*"He who lives in harmony with himself
lives in harmony with the universe."*
—Marcus Aurelius

T he universal law of vibration speaks to us of how we tap into the power of love. Our thoughts and actions have a ripple effect on those we come into contact with. Without that ripple, love is stagnant. We need a means to carry that love from person to person.

We are like a bridge that carries this vibration to every soul on the planet. Our actions either have a positive or negative effect on how we are perceived.

Have you ever met someone for the first time and felt uneasy around them? You have encountered a negative vibration in the area of love. Not everyone has positive vibrations. Many people try to hide their negativity and it is only later do we find out who they really are. If we're not careful, we can be fooled into thinking we care about these people only to find we get caught up in their web of lies and deceit.

This is the main cause of disruption in our accessing true love. This disruption causes pain and unhappiness and we lose our access to love. Sometimes, we are the cause with our actions and our negativity which pushes love away. Just like gravity pulls things down, our actions and negativity bring us down. It can be hard to rejuvenate our hearts and minds when this happens and we become fixated on depressing types of behavior.

Thought is the most potent vibration known to man because the energy it produces can change anything you want. Altering your thoughts and emotions can produce the kind of change that brings love. Unfortunately, most of us worry far too much about things we cannot change such as money, fear, the past, and our own limitations. When you change your thought patterns and your feelings (emotions) you attract the type of love that transforms your life and bring about real happiness.

You may think that money can change your life for the better but it won't if you don't change your thoughts first. You will still have the same problems you had before only now money will become a crutch to lean on.

Positive action must be applied in order for us to manifest love on earth. Therefore, engage in positive actions that support your thoughts, your emotions, and most importantly, your words. Words are energy that either hurt or uplift others. Use your words carefully and let love give you the right words to say at the right time.

Vibration is based on the idea that positive energies attract positive energies and negative energies attract negative energies. Love is the embodiment of positive energy, for love cannot exist and function where negativity reigns. There must be a balance for this to happen.

When we find balance in our lives we look for a real transformation. This transformation is full of energy that can bring an inner joy and peace which allows love to blossom. When you unlock the inner peace and joy within, you can boost your energy, your stamina, and vitality making it easier to attract positive love.

Living a life from the heart means giving your energy the freedom to express itself. But remember, you need to shift your vibrational energy to become both a transmitter and a receiver so that you can access true love.

If you are only open to receiving love then you are muting the vibration. Open your heart so it can flow both ways.

Everything works together for the goodness of love but attracting love is driven by vision. You attract what are signaling the universe. You either repel or attract what you are in harmony with.

Let me give you an example of this. If you physically radiate self-confidence people will be attracted to you. If you physically radiate anger or hate you will repel others. Change your signals and you will attract what you want.

Not attracting good things in your life?

Here's how to change your vibration and start attracting what is important in your life.

Concentrate on the things you want such as love friendship, money, a good job, and better health. Keep those thoughts strong in your mind and make them positive. Whenever you feel like you don't deserve them, channel the positive thoughts back into your mind. Believe that you already have them and live like you are in possession of them. You will start attracting your dreams much quicker.

Remember, those things all come from God so keep Him strong in your heart. When you combine a strong faith in God with a positive outlook on life, the things you want start appearing as you need them.

Want to attract friendship? Be a good friend. Want to attract happiness? Become a happy person.

To become what you want, you need to create balance and harmony in everything you do. Too much chaos destroys the balance of nature. The energy you produce is the cause of all your experiences. This where unconditional love can help you balance your life's vibrational energy and help you receive grace and give mercy to others.

This is why we work so hard to gain friendships, love, and peace in our lives. We all want results but it takes effort on our part. You are not going to be handed everything on a silver platter. You need to go out and attract the things you want.

Want to live in harmony with God's love? According to **Ayya Khema** from his book**, "Be an Island - The Buddhist Practice of Inner Peace,"** he writes, *"What we create in the world becomes a mirror image of what we find in ourselves."*

Do you see how being in harmony can create the type of love we need in our life? Love is not a matter of wanting but of doing, or in this case, creating the ideal environment to foster love. Harmony is at the core of happiness.

He goes on to say, *"Contentment in our hearts is rooted in emotional independence, in giving love and approval rather than trying to get them."*

Our whole lives have been contingent upon our going after approval instead of giving love and not expecting anything in return.

It has been said that if you have no peace in your heart you have nothing in your life. When we practice peace in everything we do, harmony soon follows. When we are full of harmony, our lives are balanced. We then have the power to give our love unconditionally without feeling like we are owed something in return. Small acts of kindness will not be in vain but will add to the happiness of others.

Peace is all based on balance… a balance in our minds, a balance in our emotions, a balance in our hearts, and balance in our work and play. The Persian poet, **Hafiz**, expresses what balance is in our lives by stating *"I wish I could show you when you are lonely or in darkness, the Astonishing Light of your own being."*

That light brings us closer to God and sends harmony to our lives.

HOW TO BE A MAGNET FOR LOVE

"There is a magnet in your heart that will attract true friends. That magnet is unselfishness, thinking of others first; when you learn to live for others, they will live for you."
—Paramahansa Yogananda

D o you live in love?
Do you live for others?
Paramahansa Yogananda has taught me so much about myself, especially how to live a life of loving kindness. I have become strong in my faith but even stronger in my love. He states that, *"As a mortal being you are limited, but as a child of God you are unlimited... Focus your attention on God, and you shall have all the power you want, to use in any direction."*

Love has become a real passion with me. I'm passionate about helping others transform their lives and find a deeper and more lasting love. I've become a magnet for love without really trying because people pick up on my energy and my enthusiasm, whether consciously or subconsciously. It's all about radiating confidence in others.

The people who are attracted to me are a reflection of who I am. My whole life before my accident was full of disharmony. There was no peace in my heart and my life was a series of haphazard events that brought no happiness to me or to the people I came in contact with. I wasn't attracting anyone... I was pushing them away.

When I was eight years old, we moved to the Pocono Mountains in Pennsylvania from our home on the Jersey Shore. Back then, the Poconos were sparsely populated and our home was a mile from the nearest house. I was lonely, scared, and felt so unloved.

For my parents, it was a last go-round to see if they could resurrect their marriage but it didn't quite work out. Hope seemed like a lost cause. It was a miserable time but I look back on that time as a watershed in my life as it was the beginning of my love for writing. Forty five years later, the loneliness I felt back then has manifested itself in such a beautiful way.

My writing gives me joy and hope to others. The love I have for writing emanates in how I treat others. I look to inspire others with my gift and show my love in everything I do.

Becoming a magnet for love is conveyed in how you touch other people's hearts. Having an impact on others brings you more love and more happiness into your life but it's even more amazing what it does for others. People will do almost anything for love but when they see someone who is authentic they will be much more inclined to open themselves up to being loved.

What you believe in you will achieve. If you believe you are worthy of love, you will have it. If you believe you deserve to be loved, you will be loved. When you are kind and gentle to yourself, you will be kind and gentle to others. This in turn, will bring kindness and gentleness back to you.

Did you know that your natural state of being is a state of love? Being in a state of fear blocks us from that natural state. If you are conscious of what you think, feel, and do, you will be more in tune to attracting what you want in life. Pay attention to life and you will see more love than you could ever know.

Ken Page, L.C.S.W., a New York based psychotherapist, author and lecturer says this about being a magnet for love, *"The first step was almost always the same: The choice to spend time with what I call "attractions of inspiration," those friends and partners with whom there is an essential sense of safety and mutual appreciation, and gradually spending less and less time with "attractions of deprivation," those relationships which require inordinate* *effort to get the other person to accept us, appreciate us, and honor who we really are."*

If you concentrate on building deeper relationships with people who uplift you, you learn to be happy long before you look for relationships to make you happy.

Are you are willing to take action on your own behalf to bring yourself happiness?

Don't be dependent on others to do this for you. Your genuine happiness will attract likeminded people who are also making themselves happy. This opens the door to a attracting more love into your life.

In his book entitled **"The Rules Of Love: A Personal Code For Happier, More Fulfilling Relationships"**, author **Richard Templar** gives an good idea of how to attract more love into our lives, *"The universe doesn't always give back love from where you gave it. Your generosity to one person may be returned by a complete stranger. But if you keep putting it out wherever you see that it's needed, you'll keep getting it back in buckets."*

Why is this so? Those that give always receive more than they give out and so it is with being a magnet for love. The more love you give out the more it shall be returned during your lifetime.

There are times in our lives when we are meant to be a blessing for others. We are meant to be in that time and space to help someone but if we fail to recognize our role, we miss that precious opportunity to build bridges of love.

I know I still have a lot of catching up to do when it comes to giving out love but that's the beauty here. You just need to start. It doesn't matter what happened before. It all starts now!

Love and be loved. Depend on Jesus for everything and live as if it is your last day on earth and you will see the healing that you so desperately need. It doesn't get any easier than that.

The love we have is free to give. It is the compass that points to our greatest asset; our ability to be unselfish. We have a commitment to share that love with the whole world in a way that lifts everyone up at the same time, not just ourselves.

We must assume the responsibility to care for love, nurture it as it grows in others, and respect the power it has to bring people together. God has given you a mighty gift. Use it to the best of your ability then spread it to the ends of the earth. Love is special. Don't let it go by without getting a taste.

When you become a magnet for love, you are vowing to put God's love first and allowing him to use you in the lives of others. To attract love like a magnet you must give love like your own life depends on it survival. **Winston Churchill** once said, "*We make a living by what we get, but we make a life by what we give.*"

Give till hurts... and then keep on giving more. You'll be surprised by how much love changes you for the better!

A FINAL THOUGHT

*"In order to be an image of God, the spirit must
turn to what is eternal, hold it in spirit, keep it in
memory, and by loving it, embrace it in the will."*
—Edith Stein

I f anyone should have lost at love it should have been me. I was the poster
child for failing at life and everything associated with it but that didn't faze
God. Not at all! He has used me to bring hope to others just like me and help
guide them to a new path in life.

The former First Lady, **Eleanor Roosevelt** once remarked, *"We are afraid
to care too much, for fear that the other person does not care at all."* Take
it from me, never be afraid to care too much. It's caring too little that gets you
in trouble.

When you are lost in your fears you have no capacity to find love. It
is physically impossible. Tackle you fears head on and you will find the inner

strength that God has given you. You have the keys to this great mystery in which God has placed before you.

In her bestselling Book, **"You Can Heal Your Life,"** author **Louise L. Hay** wrote this about dealing with others, *"Relationships are mirrors of ourselves. What we attract always mirrors either qualities we have or beliefs we have about relationships."* Healing comes when we change our thought patterns.

I never thought I was worthy to be loved but now I am so full of love it's a joy to give it unconditionally. I used to believe I wasn't good enough for anyone or anything but I've been blessed with so much from God and I want to share it with you.

If you're lying there in bed, tears streaming down your cheeks because you've been hurt and you feel unwanted, unloved, and unworthy, remember, I was there too. I felt those same feelings. I lived that same life but now I'm giving you the chance to transform yours.

I believe you are worthy, I believe you are loved, and I believe you are important. No matter what others say or feel about you God knows the real you and wants to heal you. He's never been wrong about anyone and he won't be wrong about you.

Look, God saved my life and showed me His great love. I've changed how I act towards others and how I think which has given me a second chance. I have peace in my soul and wish to share it with you.

Each day is a day to cherish your life. It's a day to find love in all the small things. Happiness comes from that love and I want to help you find and keep it.

The only way life is going to change for you is if you put into action everything you have learned here. It took me years to understand that. It took a devastating car accident to get my attention. Don't let things get that bad for you.

Learn from me how to harness the true power of love so that you can heal your broken life. I can only show you the path but the change must come from deep inside of you.

Now that you have the 3 step solution to bring more love into your life in your hands, it's up to you to take the next step. Don't be like others who only read and take no action at all.

I've been through a lot and don't want to pass up what this life has to offer me. Love matters and so do you. I know you want to do this but you may be feeling scared, have lingering doubts, maybe even want to spare yourself some long ago heartache you can't quite bear but that's the beauty of love. You don't know what to expect. Well, just trust your heart…it never lies.

If I am to love others I have a great example to live by. God asks us to embrace his love and through this love we are to pass it on. I am passing my love on to you. Take it and then pass it on to others. Don't think about it or even try to understand it. Instead, give it freely and pray that what you have done will help someone along their own journey.

Love may well be a fickle beast but time and experience heals all wounds (if you let them). We all have our own moments of unfulfillment but now is the time to find a way to make those moments last by bringing a little love of your own back into this world.

There's plenty of more room for everyone to love. Don't think you haven't been called… because you have. You just haven't heard the calling until now.

I'm calling you out and asking you to come and take the journey with me… a journey that will take you out of your comfort zone and on to a life where you can experience love in all its grandeur and beauty. A love that will change your very soul!

You need a clear vision and a clear plan. Use these steps I have written about and you'll soon be on your way. These three steps are crucial to experiencing love on a much grander scale.

I leave you with this one final thought. May you understand what it means to be loved more and may you go out and give as much love as possible to others. There is nothing else you need to do.

ABOUT THE AUTHOR

Barry Ferguson is a man on mission. Having twice survived a near-fatal car accident, God has called him to be an example of inspiration to others to help heal their own broken lives. He specializes in mind, body and spiritual health and has been interviewed on over 150 radio stations across the United States and Canada.

Despite his many failures in life, he has picked himself up and learned from his mistakes to help others do the same. He believes that everyone deserves to be loved and will not stop until he spreads his message of unconditional love throughout the world.

He is the author of over thirty books that deal with helping people in all walks of life become healthy in body, mind and spirit. His love of children has led him to diversify into the children's book market where he inspires kids with his many adventure stories.

A noted lecturer and speaker in his home state of New Jersey, he is bringing his message of hope and faith to his new weekly podcast entitled, **"Transformational Love."**

He has been married for over 25 years and has been blessed with three beautiful children who teach him everyday what true love is all about. He is a committed Christian and brings a vast knowledge of the Bible to his writings and lectures.

For more information please visit:

http://www.BarryFergusonAuthor.com

A free eBook edition
is available with the
purchase of this book.

To claim your free eBook edition:

1. Download the Shelfie app.
2. Write your name in upper case in the box.
3. Use the Shelfie app to submit a photo.
4. Download your eBook to any device.

Shelfie

A free eBook edition is available
with the purchase of this print book.

CLEARLY PRINT YOUR NAME ABOVE IN UPPER CASE

Instructions to claim your free eBook edition:
1. Download the Shelfie app for Android or iOS
2. Write your name in **UPPER CASE** above
3. Use the Shelfie app to submit a photo
4. Download your eBook to any device

Print & Digital Together Forever.

Snap a photo

Free eBook

Read anywhere

The Morgan James Speakers Group

Morgan James makes all of our titles available
through the Library for All Charity Organizations.

www.LibraryForAll.org